Capitalism, Corporations and the Social Contract

A Critique of Stakeholder Theory

In whose interests should a corporation be run? Over the last thirty years the field of 'stakeholder theory' has proposed a distinctive answer: a corporation should be run in the interests of all its primary stakeholders – including employees, customers, suppliers and financiers – without contradicting the ethical principles on which capitalism stands. This book offers a critique of this central claim. It argues that by applying the political concept of a 'social contract' to the corporation, stakeholder theory in fact undermines the principles on which a market economy is based. The argument builds upon an extensive review of the stakeholder literature and an analysis of its philosophical foundations, particularly concerning the social contract tradition of John Rawls and his predecessors. The book concludes by offering a qualified version of Milton Friedman's shareholder theory as a more justifiable account of the purpose of a corporation.

SAMUEL F. MANSELL is Lecturer in Business Ethics at the University of St Andrews. Samuel's research interests lie in the application of political and moral philosophy to the field of business ethics, with particular reference to the work of Aristotle, Aquinas, Hobbes and Kant. He is currently researching the roles of distributive justice and beneficence in the modern corporation.

Business, Value Creation and Society

Series editors
R. Edward Freeman, *University of Virginia*
Jeremy Moon, *Nottingham University*
Mette Morsing, *Copenhagen Business School*

The purpose of this innovative series is to examine, from an international standpoint, the interaction of business and capitalism with society. In the twenty-first century it is more important than ever that business and capitalism come to be seen as social institutions that have a great impact on the welfare of human society around the world. Issues such as globalization, environmentalism, information technology, the triumph of liberalism, corporate governance and business ethics all have the potential to have major effects on our current models of the corporation and the methods by which value is created, distributed and sustained among all stakeholders – customers, suppliers, employees, communities and financiers.

Published titles:

Fort *Business, Integrity, and Peace*
Gomez and Korine *Entrepreneurs and Democracy*
Crane, Matten, and Moon *Corporations and Citizenship*
Painter-Morland *Business Ethics as Practice*
Yaziji and Doh *NGOs and Corporations*
Rivera *Business and Public Policy*
Sachs and Rühli *Stakeholders Matter*

Forthcoming titles:

Maak and Pless *Responsible Leadership*
Hemingway *Corporate Social Entrepreneurship*
Hartman *Virtue in Business*

Capitalism, Corporations and the Social Contract

A Critique of Stakeholder Theory

SAMUEL F. MANSELL

CAMBRIDGE
UNIVERSITY PRESS

191902

CAMBRIDGE UNIVERSITY PRESS
Cambridge, New York, Melbourne, Madrid, Cape Town,
Singapore, São Paulo, Delhi, Mexico City

Cambridge University Press
The Edinburgh Building, Cambridge CB2 8RU, UK

Published in the United States of America by Cambridge University Press, New York

www.cambridge.org
Information on this title: www.cambridge.org/9781107015524

First published 2013

Printed and bound in the United Kingdom by the MPG Books Group

A catalog record for this publication is available from the British Library

Library of Congress Cataloging in Publication data
Mansell, Samuel F.
Capitalism, corporations and the social contract : a critique of stakeholder theory /
Samuel F. Mansell.
    pages   cm. – (Business, value creation, and society)
Includes bibliographical references and index.
ISBN 978-1-107-01552-4
1. Social responsibility of business.   2. Social contract.   3. Capitalism – Moral and
ethical aspects.   I. Title.
HD60.M36465   2013
174 – dc23   2012032863

ISBN 978-1-107-01552-4 Hardback

Contents

Foreword

A new story about business and capitalism has emerged in the last thirty years. The bare bones of this story are that every business has a set of stakeholders: groups and individuals who can affect or be affected by the purpose and operations of the business. For a business to be successful it must pay attention to these stakeholders, and ultimately it must create value for them, though sometimes value is in fact destroyed. Also, the new narrative embraces the view that human beings are complex creatures who sometimes act in their self-interest and sometimes act in regard to others. The new story eschews imputing a singular motivation to all human activity in business. Capitalism itself is essentially a system of social cooperation whereby we create and trade value together. No one of us could accomplish alone what our businesses and their stakeholders are able to create together.

This story has developed as a counterpoint to the standard modern-day narrative of capitalism as a system whose only concern is the generation of profits for owners or shareholders, and as a system that is based on greed, money and self-interest. All too often in today's post-financial-crisis world, we see more and more evidence of the power of this dominant narrative.

As "stakeholder theory" (as this new narrative has come to be called) has developed, there have been a number of variations on it, each with somewhat different assumptions, framings, and claims. The time is ripe for a more critical analysis of these theories.

Sam Mansell has produced a fine critical analysis of stakeholder theory. He is both a skeptical and a sympathetic critic, a difficult road to follow, yet the results are a fine example of how to give the best possible interpretation of a position before one begins to criticize it. More importantly, he does not examine the claims of stakeholder theory only from the standpoint of the standard narrative, where they are bound to come up short, and in error. Rather, he wonders whether stakeholder theory goes far enough both as a way to understand business practice and as an analysis of how business practice and theory need to change.

As one of many authors of this new narrative about business, I cannot pretend to be an uninterested bystander. Much of this book is critical of positions that I have held and continue to advocate. However, Mansell's critique has the potential to make stakeholder theory better and stronger. And the scholarly life demands that we pay sharp attention to our critics, to advance our knowledge in general and business practice in particular.

My hope is that this book will be one of many more to come that will help up develop a better version of stakeholder theory and continue to make business and capitalism a system of value creation and trade that is truly fit for human beings.

R. Edward Freeman
The Darden School, University of Virginia
Charlottesville, Virginia

Acknowledgements

The process of researching and writing this book has depended to a great extent on the continuing inspiration and support of a number of people. I am deeply grateful to all who have given their time and encouragement since the ideas of this book began to take shape more than six years ago. However, there are certain individuals to whom I owe a particular debt.

First, my thanks go to the supervisors of the PhD on which this book is based. Steffen Böhm provided me with the initial encouragement to do a PhD, and then at crucial stages of the process his guidance provided a direction to my work that it could easily have lost. Through the example of his own writing and extensive annotations on mine, Harro Höpfl has been an exemplar for the highest standards of scholarship. I am particularly grateful for his active support during the three years it has taken to bring the book to publication after the PhD had been completed. I would also like to thank David Weir and Bob Wearing, the examiners of the original thesis, both for their astute examination and for their encouragement to develop and publish the research.

Next I must thank my PhD colleagues at the University of Essex for their support during the years over which the majority of this research was conducted. A piece of writing on this scale throws up many personal and intellectual challenges, and in facing them the friendship and good character of my closest peers has meant a lot. My gratitude goes to Sumohon Matilal, Przemyslaw Piatkowski, Lorena Ruiz Garcia, Achilleas Karayiannis, Tom Vine and Michal Izak. I would like to acknowledge a number of past and present colleagues at Essex Business School and the University of St Andrews for creating a stimulating environment for teaching and research. In particular, my thanks go to John Desmond, Nick Butler, Philip Roscoe, Rob Gray, Jan Bebbington, Heather Höpfl, Chris Land, Hardy Thomas, Marjana Johansson and Lee Parker, who all offered valuable insight and support at various stages of the book's completion.

My thanks also go to my colleagues at the Centre for Philosophy and Political Economy at the University of Leicester. The opportunity to become an outside member of this unique research community and to present my work annually at their *Symposium* has greatly enriched my experience of writing the book. I'd like to acknowledge Armin Beverungen, Eleni Karamali, Jeroen Veldman and in particular Stephen Dunne, whom it has been fantastic to work with in some exciting areas of research.

At Cambridge University Press, I am especially grateful to Paula Parish for giving my project the benefit of the doubt when its prospects were undecided, and then for steering it through every stage of the publication process with consummate professionalism. My thanks go to the series editor, Ed Freeman, for his crucial support of the project and his timely and constructive advice in revising the text. Two anonymous reviewers and the series advisers – Luc van Liedekerke, Jeremy Moon and Mette Morsing – all took the time to offer detailed feedback on the entire book, for which I am very grateful. Furthermore, I would like to thank William Stoddard for his meticulous work in copy-editing the manuscript.

I also acknowledge Edward Elgar for their permission to reproduce part of my chapter 'Business Ethics and the Question of Objectivity: The Concept of Moral Progress in a Dialectical Framework', in Muhr, S., Sørensen, B. and Vallentin, S. (eds.) *Ethics and Organizational Practice: Questioning the Moral Foundations of Management* (2010).

Beyond academia, I owe a lot to the close friends I am fortunate to have had from before I started this project, who never failed to give me support and (most importantly) perspective during the most difficult times of writing. My sincerest thanks to Paras Mehta, Alan Rattenbury, Yang Hu, Stojan Kitanov, Ben Outram and Jono Beasley. I would also like to thank Kevin Stowe, Leon van Oudheusden and Antonio Gil Asenjo, who showed me that the activity of a philosopher is a vocation worth having.

My continuing gratitude goes to my family, whose love and support have been crucial in making this book possible in the first place. My heartfelt thanks to my parents Rick and Nerys Mansell, to my brothers

Ben and James Mansell, to Miriam Chilton, and to my grandfather Norman Hughes. Above all, my principal thanks are for my fiancée, Edzia Carvalho. Her unwavering love and support have been the cornerstone of everything I have achieved since our first conversation, back in 2009, on the very day I submitted this thesis.

1 | Introduction

In recent years an undeniable characteristic of the political discourse of developed nations has been an increased focus on the ethics of the modern business corporation. Since the mid-1990s, the public controversies surrounding the 'McLibel' trial,[1] Royal Dutch Shell's disposal of its Brent Spar platform and role in the execution of Nigerian activist Ken Saro-Wiwa,[2] and the accounting scandals of Enron and WorldCom in the United States and Ahold and Parmalat in Europe have been amongst numerous examples of growing public concern over the unethical practices of business corporations. Today, issues of bank lending in the sub-prime mortgage crisis and (following publicly funded bailouts) the level of bonuses paid to bank executives, as well as continuing environmental degradation, tax avoidance and the exploitation of cheap labour in developing countries, lead many to ask what the social role of the corporation should be and what responsibilities it has. The increasing portion of the global economy directly under the control of corporations has also caused an ethical outcry and led to calls for corporations to be held democratically to account in the same manner as national governments.[3]

---

[1] The colloquial term given to the court action for libel brought by McDonald's Restaurants against environmental activists Helen Steel and David Morris, in response to a pamphlet published by the activists which criticised McDonald's, inter alia, for exploiting its work force, selling unhealthy food, being cruel to animals and using unethical marketing practices. It developed into the longest-running court case in English history.

[2] Donaldson and Dunfee (1999: 1–5), in *Ties That Bind*, give a good overview of this incident and the changes it led to in Shell's approach to corporate social responsibility.

[3] Mitchell and Sikka, writing in 2005, had already pointed to the fact that some 60% of world trade was within multinational corporations and the largest hundred corporations controlled 20% of global foreign assets, to illustrate the economic power wielded by corporations and the need to limit their powers through the institutions of democracy (2005: 3). This idea also forms a central part of Bakan's (2004) argument in his book *The Corporation*.

In short, the role of the business corporation in contemporary society is a strongly contested issue, and it is perhaps impossible to have an opinion on political life today without holding a position on it. Given its prevalence as a matter of public concern and the tangible role that corporations play in the lives of almost everyone living in market-based societies, the precise way this issue is understood is a matter of more than intellectual curiosity. In democratic societies where policies largely reflect public opinion, the general interpretation of the social role of the corporation directly affects the overall organisation of society, and potentially the life prospects of all who depend on corporations for necessary goods and services. It follows that any theory which can influence the way this problem is perceived is potentially of great importance.

An example of this is the currently popular body of ideas known as 'stakeholder theory'. Stakeholder theory holds, largely as a response to the kind of ethical controversies outlined in the preceding, that the primary responsibility of a corporation is not to maximise shareholder wealth, but instead to serve the interests of a range of stakeholders that make up the society in which it operates. These stakeholders are taken to include not merely the shareholders, but employees, lenders, suppliers, the local community and even 'society' at large. Though disagreements exist over exactly which stakeholders are to be considered legitimate, the idea that a corporation's objective should encompass the interests of non-shareholding groups is held as a fundamental step in establishing an ethically responsible business outlook.

Stakeholder theory plays a valuable role in highlighting the importance of theorising about the social responsibilities of business and of generating academic debate on this issue, of which this book is a product. It also offers a compelling alternative to two sharply opposed positions, one of which sees the profit-making nature of the corporation as a commercial vehicle as disastrous for society as a whole (Bakan 2004), while the other sees the maximisation of shareholder wealth as the only legitimate objective that a corporation can pursue in a market economy (e.g., Friedman 1962, 1970). However, while stakeholder theory no doubt stimulates valuable debate on these issues, the aim of this book is to examine the conceptual coherence of the theory itself. The theory in its current form seems to assume a harmonious relationship of elements between which, in actuality, choices must be made.

My hypothesis is that a number of positions are advocated which, while of ethical value in themselves, are found upon inspection to be irreconcilable with each other.

What follows is therefore not an empirical study of the effects of corporate behaviour on stakeholders, or the effect of stakeholder theory upon the actions of corporate managers. Nor am I primarily concerned with its relationship to other theories of business or other avenues of corporate social responsibility (CSR). Though these are important areas of enquiry, my argument is aimed at the structure of the theory itself. I proceed by making an abstraction of the elements that can be considered essential to it, in order to outline the conceptual framework with which any version of stakeholder theory must be consistent. I then work through an analysis of these concepts to see whether a realisation of the theory is possible without the emergence of logical contradictions. The central question raised is whether any goals can be pursued by a corporation in a market-based economy that are not reducible to the interests of shareholders, given that an acceptance of the basic moral framework of capitalism is a premise widely shared by defenders of stakeholder theory. This book is chiefly concerned with a critical analysis of the consistency of this position. The question turns out to depend on whether the corporation is seen as a commercial entity existing for the sole purpose of market exchange, or as a political entity with sovereign rights over its stakeholders analogous to the relationship between a state and its citizens.[4] However, before summarising the stages of the argument, the importance of stakeholder theory can be gauged by placing it in the context of two popular but radically opposed discourses on the social responsibility of the corporation.

Competing perspectives on corporate responsibility

A prevailing interpretation of recent corporate scandals is that morally responsible business conduct is impossible as long as corporations remain accountable to their shareholders alone. It is argued that if

---

[4] This is not to suggest that any corporation involved in politics, for example, through lobbying or contracting with governments, necessarily has sovereign rights. The question is whether corporations should be understood *essentially* as political entities in relation to their stakeholders, with their responsibilities justified on this basis.

the maximisation of profits is the only legitimate objective for business, then the exercise of responsibility towards other 'stakeholders' is
unobtainable. The pursuit of shareholder wealth maximisation is primarily to blame, by this reasoning, for the recent string of accounting
scandals and other ethical failures. Businesses can be expected to work
for the public good only when this view is abandoned and management can adopt social objectives that are not reducible to maximising
shareholder wealth.

This identification of corporate scandals with shareholder wealth
maximisation receives one of its best-known expressions in the book
The Corporation (and the accompanying film) by Joel Bakan. For
Bakan, the implications of the shareholder view are as follows:

Corporations have only one duty: to promote their own and their owners'
interests. They have no capacity, and their executives no authority, to act
out of a genuine sense of responsibility to society, to avoid causing harm to
people and the environment, or to work to advance the public good in ways
that are unrelated to their own self-interest. (Bakan 2004: 109)

As a result, Bakan (2004: 2) argues, 'the corporation is a pathological
institution, a dangerous possessor of the great power it wields over
people and societies'. He writes that ever since the creation of the
modern business corporation (with limited liability) in the middle of
the nineteenth century, it has remained 'a legally designated "person"
designed to valorise self-interest and invalidate moral concern. Most
people would find its "personality" abhorrent, even psychopathic, in a
human being, and yet curiously we accept it in society's most powerful
institution' (2004: 28). The connection Bakan sees between the legally
defined mandate of the corporation (to pursue shareholder value as
its only objective) and its 'psychopathic' disregard for any harm it
might cause in this process implies that for him the explanation for
corporate scandals must be this objective to act for the shareholders
alone. Therefore, in assessing the reasons for the collapse of Enron, he
writes:

Though the company is now notorious for its arrogance and ethically challenged executives, the underlying reasons for its collapse can be traced
to characteristics common to all corporations: obsession with profits and
share prices, greed, lack of concern for others, and a penchant for breaking
legal rules. These traits are, in turn, rooted in an institutional culture, the

corporation's, that valorises self-interest and invalidates moral concern. (Bakan 2004: 58)

The NGO Corporate Watch reaches a similar verdict in a report entitled *What's Wrong with Corporate Social Responsibility?* It argues that as a corporation is under a legal obligation to maximise profits, it is incapable of taking any wider public interest into account. Therefore, 'the wider social good can only ever be incidental to the interest of making a profit. This is a total reversal of conventional moral priorities that place the interests of society over self-interest' (Corporate Watch 2006: 11). In an argument similar to that of Bakan (2004), the report goes on to claim: 'Corporations have highly destructive impacts on society and the environment, and they are the dominant institution in our society, so if the only type of actions that they can make to mitigate their destructive impacts are the most profitable ones, then prospects for the planet do not look good' (ibid.).

Holding the shareholder view responsible for corporate scandals is a position also common to advocates of stakeholder theory. Robert Phillips (2003), in *Stakeholder Theory and Organizational Ethics*, the first book-length normative defence of stakeholder theory, writes:

No small measure of managerial opportunism has occurred in the name of shareholder wealth maximisation. In addition to the debacles of Enron and WorldCom, one need only consider the now dethroned king of shareholder wealth, Al Dunlap...Dunlap grossly mismanaged at least two companies to his own significant, if temporary, financial gain; and every move he made was in the name of shareholder wealth. (Phillips 2003: 20)

Freeman et al. (2004) propound a similar view. In response to the charge that having more than one objective function (as stakeholder theory advocates) makes governance and management difficult, they declare: 'It is hard to imagine how anyone can look at the recent wave of business scandals, all of which are oriented toward ever-increasing shareholder value at the expense of other stakeholders, and argue that this philosophy is a good idea' (Freeman et al. 2004: 366). The assumption appears widely held that a causal relationship between the pursuit of shareholder wealth and morally opprobrious business conduct is a good explanation for the egregious scandals that have recently enveloped the business world.

In tandem with this view it is often argued, though *not* by stake-holder theorists (as shall be shown later), that a meaningful remedy for the ethical failures of corporations is impossible in the context of the market institutions in which they operate. A necessary condition for alleviating the damage done to society by the corporation is assumed to be a complete reform of the market economy. Bakan (2004: 160), for example, asks, 'should all corporations become public-purpose corporations? Is that the solution to our current corporate woes?' He goes on to say that such a solution, even if desirable, is too utopian at present to be a realistic option, but writes: 'Perhaps someday we shall understand how truly to democratise economic relations, and widespread use of public-purpose corporations may be a key part of the plan' (Bakan 2004: 160–1). Likewise, Corporate Watch states that a meaningful level of social responsibility 'is not something a corporation, as corporations are currently structured, could handle. It is not within its world view. Society must create new structures to replace corporations, ones that could operate in a way that might meet [socially responsible] criteria' (2006: 24). Clearly as a solution to failures of corporate ethics this is an advocacy not merely of corporate reform, but of an upheaval of the entire economic system itself.

There is, however, a competing discourse which takes a very different view on the moral implications of acting for shareholder interests, but with an important similarity with regard to the economic context in which business operates. It is argued that the adoption by managers of any objective *other* than the maximisation of shareholder wealth is a subversion of the basic framework of a market economy and the very idea of a 'free society'. To pursue objectives which may be desirable from the perspective of 'society' or the 'public interest', but are in conflict with the interests of shareholders, would be a violation of the ethical principles that any market-based society has to recognise. This is the argument of Milton Friedman (1962, 1970), perhaps the best-known critic of CSR. The claim that a socially responsible business must not act other than to maximise shareholder wealth is clearly the opposite of the first perspective outlined. However, the assumption that a deviation from this purpose, if permitted generally, would undermine the basic framework of a market economy is common to both perspectives.

One of Friedman's central arguments is that the duty of management to pursue shareholder interests as its sole objective is founded upon ethical principles that are fundamental to a market economy, and that must be accepted by anyone for whom business plays a legitimate role in such an economy. He writes: 'In an ideal free market resting on private property, no individual can coerce any other, all cooperation is voluntary, all parties to such cooperation benefit or they need not participate' (1970). His view of business is that shareholders voluntarily entrust their private property to management, on the expectation that management will act so as to maximise the value of this property, and it is a violation of their property rights if managers pursue contrary objectives. He asserts:

The businessmen believe they are defending free enterprise when they declaim that business is not concerned 'merely' with profit but also with promoting desirable 'social' ends.... In fact they are – or would be if they or anyone else took them seriously – preaching pure and unadulterated socialism. Businessmen who talk this way are unwitting puppets of the intellectual forces that have been undermining the basis of a free society these past decades. (Ibid.)

A prominent critic of stakeholder theory in recent years, Elaine Sternberg, expounds a similar view. She writes that for management to pursue social objectives with the money of shareholders would undermine two fundamental features of 'modern society': 'private property and the duties that agents owe to principals. The stakeholder doctrine undermines private property, because it denies owners the right to determine how their property will be used' (Sternberg 2004: 147).

This perspective, which defends the 'shareholder theory' of the firm, stands in marked contrast to the competing idea that this outlook is largely responsible for the ethical crises of business. Instead, it is asserted that far from being ethically culpable, the shareholder view is the *only* ethically acceptable model of the corporation, as long as the legitimacy of a market economy is assumed. However, in both cases, it is held that if one *does* assume the context of a market economy, then one cannot expect the business corporation to have any other purpose than to maximise shareholder wealth. There is of course a scale of opinions on this issue, and the brief citations offered here represent merely the opposite poles rather than the full range. However, given the key similarity between these positions, whether one takes a view favourable to one side or the other, the question of how a corporation can be socially responsible depends ultimately on the merits of rival economic and political systems. Either the basic economic and moral framework of a market economy is upheld or it is overturned. So the problem of CSR is made to depend not on what a corporation can do *within* an economic system, but on which overall political philosophy is justifiable. The striking feature of *stakeholder theory* is that it aims to show that a business can exercise social responsibility through a purpose irreducible to shareholder objectives, *without* contradicting the moral framework of a capitalist economy. Standing to reconcile the concerns of both the positions so far expounded, stakeholder theory appears to offer a compelling alternative.

Contrasting stakeholder and shareholder theories

A brief survey of the various definitions of stakeholder theory shows basic similarities across its different forms. Wijnberg (2000: 329) writes: 'In its most basic sense, stakeholder theory arises from the rejection of the idea that the corporation should single-handedly strive to maximise the benefits of a single stakeholder, the shareholders'. A similar view is expressed by Mitchell et al. (1997: 855), who write that the stakeholder approach is 'intended to broaden management's vision of its roles and responsibilities beyond the profit maximisation function to include interests and claims of non-stockholding groups'. Furthermore, in an analysis of 179 articles published on stakeholder theory between 1984 and 2007, Laplume et al. (2008: 1153) find that 'A fundamental thesis of stakeholder-based arguments is that organisations should be managed in the interests of all their constituents, not only in the interest of shareholders'. A clear similarity appears to the position of Bakan (2004) and Corporate Watch (2006), in that a business cannot be ethical if it looks only to maximise shareholder value.

In a much-cited overview of the field, Donaldson and Preston (1995: 68) write: 'Stakeholder analysts argue that *all* persons or groups with legitimate interests participating in an enterprise do so to obtain benefits and . . . there is no prima facie priority of one set of interests and benefits over another'. Here there is the added specification of *legitimate interests*. A theory of what might count as a legitimate interest is therefore crucial to the stakeholder approach. Kaler (2003: 71) expounds another position common to stakeholder theorists, writing that the crucial distinction between shareholder and stakeholder theory is 'their respective rejection and acceptance of role-specific responsibilities toward non-shareholders that are "ultimate objective fulfilling"'. These summaries suggest a clear opposition between the shareholder and stakeholder approaches, in that the latter maintains that management has a responsibility to pursue stakeholder interests as ultimate objectives of the firm.

However, Freeman (2008) and Freeman et al. (2010) claim that at the pragmatic level of managerial decision-making it is a mistake to see these two perspectives as necessarily in conflict. They argue that 'maximisation of shareholder value' is impossible without the creation of value for all primary stakeholders.[5] To illustrate this point, Freeman writes that if you want to maximise returns to shareholders:

You've got to have great products and services that people want, that do what you say they are going to do. You need suppliers who want to make your company better, and who stand behind what they do. You need employees who show up and want to be there, be creative and productive. You need communities for whom you are at least a good citizen so they don't use the political process . . . to destroy the value you create. And, you have to make money for the financiers. (Freeman 2008: 165)

In short, the manager of any business has to recognise that the interests of a range of stakeholders in creating and trading value must be addressed for the business to succeed. An *exclusive* focus on profit maximisation to the detriment of the interests of non-shareholders is in fact a sure way to destroy value for all stakeholders, including shareholders. The implication is that stakeholder interests have to be shaped by the manager to go in the same direction over time. Freeman (ibid.) writes that there is a 'jointness to these interests' and 'the key idea about capitalism is that the entrepreneur or manager creates value by capturing the jointness of the interests'. This means that 'one must focus on how value gets created for each and every stakeholder' (Freeman et al. 2010: 9). For these reasons, Freeman (2008: 166) believes Friedman would agree with him that 'The primary responsibility of an executive is to create as much value as possible for stakeholders because that's how

---

[5] Freeman et al. (2010: 24) list communities, customers, employees, suppliers and financiers as 'primary stakeholders'. In their analysis a broader category of 'secondary' or 'instrumental' stakeholders who can potentially affect the achievement of an organisation's purpose include government, competitors, consumer advocate groups, special interest groups and the media (2010: 24–26).

you create as much value as possible for shareholders' (ibid.). Freeman et al. (2010: 12) add that 'Friedman's maximising shareholder value is compatible with stakeholder theory. After all, the only way to maximise value sustainably is to satisfy stakeholder interests'.

These authors argue persuasively that managers whose immediate aim is to cooperate with all stakeholders on whom the firm depends, for example, by providing good products and services for customers, and by supporting working conditions that motivate employees, will generally create more value for shareholders than managers whose *only* aim is to satisfy this latter group.[6] As Freeman (2008: 165–6) puts it, maximising profits 'is an outcome of a well-managed company' and 'stakeholder theory is an idea about what it means to be well-managed'. It might therefore be a mistake to see shareholder theory and stakeholder theory as necessarily opposed in the day-to-day management of a firm.

However, the differences between these two perspectives can be seen more clearly if one looks not at the immediate tasks necessary for running a business, but at its more fundamental, longer-term objectives. One can ask: in pursuit of what *purpose* does management require the cooperation of primary stakeholders? A business might indeed create value for its stakeholders, and find ways of satisfying their joint interests, in the pursuit of long-term aims that are not merely equivalent to the aims of all its stakeholders. Shareholder and stakeholder theorists give strongly contrasting answers to the question of whether a corporation's ultimate objective should comprise the interests of a range of stakeholders or the interests of shareholders alone.

Freeman (2008: 163) is sceptical of framing the arguments in this way. He writes, 'I tire of the debate between what really is the purpose of the firm – in other words, what are the means and what are the ends'. He cites Dewey's contention that 'means have a way of becoming ends which subsequently have a way of becoming means' (ibid.).

---

[6] This may sound like a common sense observation. However, a corporate scandal such as Enron in which an obsession with stock price at least partly explains an extravagant (and fraudulent) manipulation of accounting standards, and the subsequent collapse of the company (Cruver 2003; McLean and Elkind 2004) highlights the importance of the practical point that Freeman et al. are making.

However, in welcoming Milton Friedman 'to the big tent of stake-holder theorists', Freeman (2008: 165–6) is quick to dissociate himself from shareholder theorists' claims about the corporate purpose: 'Does that mean that I believe that "maximizing profits" is the goal or purpose of the corporation? Absolutely not'. Freeman et al. (2010: 28) are also quite clear that the central aim of business is to create as much value as possible for all stakeholders without resorting to trade-offs that prioritise one stakeholder over another. In contrast, shareholder theory holds that if trade-offs between stakeholders *do* need to be made,[7] the primary intention in making the trade-off should be to further a purpose that can be justified to shareholders. From this perspective, while cooperation with a range of stakeholders may be necessary, management is accountable for the *results* of the firm's activities to shareholders alone, and not to any non-shareholding stakeholders. Stakeholder interests therefore only 'go in the same direction' to the extent that the consequent results are acceptable to shareholders.

For an example of the difference between these two perspectives, one can imagine a company that makes a profitable return from investing in technology that happens to be destroying the natural environment in a remote part of the world without any immediate effect on its primary stakeholders. Employees, suppliers, customers, etc., are all happy to receive a share of the profit that the company is creating. However, a majority of shareholders decide to support a 'social responsibility' proposal urging the company either to withdraw its activities from this area or produce a 'sustainability report' detailing its effects on the environment. The other stakeholders are concerned that either course of action will damage the firm's profitability and reduce the value created for them. For example, suppliers might receive fewer orders, customers could be asked to pay higher prices and employees may face redundancy.

Clearly, in deciding upon an ethical strategy to adopt, managers would face a different set of obligations if they are held accountable to

---

[7] Norman Bowie (2012), in a recent review of Freeman et al.'s (2010) *Stakeholder Theory: The State of the Art*, notes that for managers to practice stakeholder theory 'without resorting to trade-offs' is a worthy ideal, but 'the necessity of trade-offs may be required more often than the authors think' (ibid.: 183).

shareholders alone, than if they are considered responsible for pursuing the interests of customers, suppliers and employees, for example. In this scenario, a shareholder theorist would argue that while managers must fulfil their contractual duties to non-shareholders and observe the general constraints of 'law and ethical custom' (Friedman, 1970), the proposal should be implemented if it has the clear support of shareholders. Stakeholder theorists, however, hold that shareholder interests have no moral priority and that the corporate purpose must reflect the support of other groups, whatever the merits of the proposal in question. The precise normative arguments used by stakeholder theorists are the subject of the next chapter, but insofar as they reject the idea that management should pursue *only* those objectives that can be justified to shareholders, the opposition with shareholder theory is most clearly seen.

Stakeholder theory and corporate social responsibility in a market economy

A clear overlap can be found between stakeholder theory and the discourse of 'corporate social responsibility' (CSR). CSR shares with the stakeholder approach an emphasis on the moral legitimacy of certain individuals/groups whose interests in the firm should be satisfied directly as corporate objectives. As Freeman et al. (2010: 40) put it, 'corporate social responsibility...can be viewed as applying the stakeholder concept to non-traditional stakeholder groups who are usually thought of as having an adversarial relationship with the firm. In particular, less emphasis is put on satisfying owners and comparatively more emphasis is put on the public, the community, or the employees'.

Tencanti et al. (2004) outline many definitions of what CSR ought to mean for business that reveal similarities to the kind of responsibilities outlined by stakeholder theorists. According to them, the first modern contribution to the topic of CSR came from Bowen (1953: 6), for whom '[CSR] refers to the obligations of businessmen to pursue those policies, to make those decisions, or to follow those lines of action which are most desirable in terms of the objectives and values of our society'. Tencanti et al. also cite a more recent source in the World Business Council for Sustainable Development (1999): 'CSR is the continuing commitment by business to behave ethically and contribute to economic development while improving the quality of life of the workforce and their families as well as of the local community and society at large' (cited in Tencanti et al. 2004: 175). Furthermore, a Green Paper drawn up by the European Union in 2001 declares: 'CSR is essentially a concept whereby companies decide voluntarily to contribute to a better society and a cleaner environment' (Commission of the European Communities, 2001: 4; cited in Tencanti et al. 2004: 176). Kaler (2006: 252) argues that CSR and the stakeholder approach to running corporations are more or less synonymous, because 'CSR is all about taking on responsibilities to society beyond those owed to shareholders and what else is this but to argue for a more extensive serving of non-shareholder interests relative to those of shareholders?'

The way I engage with stakeholder theory is to see it *not* as synonymous with CSR, but instead as a set of normative justifications for why CSR ought to be accepted as the proper outlook for corporations. This is not to suggest that stakeholder theory is the only appropriate basis for CSR. There are of course an enormous variety of applications made of the concept of social responsibility to business, and not all are versions of stakeholder theory. For example, several of the CSR theories outlined in Garriga and Melé's (2004) comprehensive overview of the field do not provide an explicit normative justification for a corporate purpose that encompasses the interests of non-shareholders.[8] However, stakeholder theory can be seen as providing a set of ethical theories for such a normative position.

This view finds support in Carroll's (1999) observation of the specificity gained by CSR from the stakeholder approach. He writes that 'the term "social" in CSR has been seen by some as vague and lacking specificity as to whom the corporation is responsible' (1999: 290), and that through the stakeholder concept the social responsibilities of corporations are personalised, 'by delineating the specific groups or persons business should consider in its CSR orientation and activities.

---

[8] An example would be an 'instrumental theory' in which 'CSR is seen only as a strategic tool to achieve economic objectives and, ultimately, wealth creation' (Garriga and Melé 2004: 53). Instrumental theories include 'strategies for achieving competitive advantages', where – following Porter and Kramer (2002) – 'investing in philanthropic activities may be the only way to improve the context of competitive advantage of a firm' (Garriga and Melé 2004: 54); and cause-related marketing, 'a form of enlightened self-interest and a win-win situation as both the company and the charitable cause receive benefits' (Garriga and Melé 2004: 55).

Thus, the stakeholder nomenclature puts "names and faces" on the societal members or groups who are most important to business and to whom it must be responsive' (ibid.). Freeman et al. (2010) agree that the term 'social' is unhelpfully vague. They in fact propose a new definition of CSR – 'company stakeholder responsibility' – which 'requires a detailed understanding of to whom exactly a firm is responsible and the nature of those responsibilities'. They posit that firms 'need the language of stakeholders to get to a more actionable level of specificity' (2010: 264).

If arguments in the field of stakeholder theory are attempts to bring precision and content to the 'social responsibilities' of business, then such an approach clearly holds the possibility of meeting the concerns of those who hold the shareholder model of profit maximisation responsible for the ethical failures of corporations. However, it may also be asked how this approach resonates with those expressing the contrary concern – that if management were to abandon shareholder wealth maximisation in favour of other objectives (supposedly closer to the 'public interest'), the very foundations of a market-based society would collapse. How indeed can stakeholder theory address this view?

A possible interpretation of the clash between stakeholder theory and its rival, shareholder theory, is that because the latter is identified with free market capitalism (e.g., through Milton Friedman's endorsement), the former might offer a critique of the free market and the political context in which business operates. As Jones et al. (2005: 97) put it: 'Typically this debate [between shareholder and stakeholder theory] ends up reinforcing rather predictable positions, in that it mirrors political divides between those for and against free, unrestrained capitalism'. However, a close look at the stakeholder literature will suggest that it is often not easy to identify the divide. Jones et al. (2005: 97) suggest that there is something 'strangely pro-capitalist in arguments for stakeholder theory' and that 'we will, once again, seek to upset the set up of this debate in business ethics'. However, the 'set up' of stakeholder theory appears to harbour no pretensions of being anti-capitalist, and few of its defenders would consider it 'strange' to be 'pro-capitalist'. Kaler (2003: 71) writes that 'the stakeholder approach involves a basically reformist stance toward capitalism, seeking . . . to move it in the direction of greater equity and a less single-minded concentration on owners' interests rather than replacing it entirely'. Kaler (2003: 79) concedes that 'there probably has to be recognition of an at least equal status for shareholder interests relative to those of any non-shareholder grouping for stakeholder theory to be about reforming rather than replacing capitalism'.

This seems to be the consistent position in stakeholder theory. Donaldson and Preston (1995: 81) write that 'the concept of a free market populated with free and rational preference seekers . . . is compatible with both stakeholder and non-stakeholder perspectives'. Donaldson (1999: 237–8) writes that stakeholder theorists of all types tend to believe in 'the compatibility of morality and capitalism', and for Jones and Wicks (1999: 622), 'an interest in practicability/profits is a sensible presumptive thesis. Indeed, this concern is so important that it ought to shape, in a fundamental way, how business is conducted'. Furthermore, Freeman and Phillips outline a 'libertarian defence' of stakeholder theory, and write that it 'countenances at most a minimal state, as defined by Nozick[9] and others' (2002: 336) and is 'distrustful of the state in any guise' (2002: 339). Freeman et al. assert that the 'real issue' is 'economic and political freedom' and make a passionate plea for seeing stakeholder theory as an inextricable part of a capitalist economy:

The shareholder ideologists want us to believe that economic freedom and therefore political freedom, are threatened by stakeholder theory. Nothing could be further from the truth. The whole idea of seeing business as the creation of value for stakeholders and the trading of that value with free consenting adults is to think about a society where each has freedom compatible with a like liberty for all (Rawls 1999). Value creation and trade have to go together.[10] (Freeman et al. 2004: 368)

Stakeholder theorists have therefore attempted to steer a path between two sharply conflicting discourses. On the one hand, they are critical of the role of the shareholder perspective in recent scandals, and

---

[9] This refers to Nozick's (1974) *Anarchy, State and Utopia*, in which the role of the state is limited to protection of individuals from violence and fraud, the awarding of compensation in the case of the violation of an individual's rights, and the enforcement of contracts.

[10] This perspective is shared by Freeman et al. (2007: viii), who write that 'we need a framework of "managing for stakeholders" in order to continue the incredible value creation engine that is capitalism'. Freeman (2008: 163) elsewhere describes himself as a 'capitalist and diehard libertarian who believes in human freedom and hope, and community solidarity, as two sides of the same coin'. Following the financial crisis, Freeman et al. (2010: 11) propose that stakeholder theory be seen as 'the basis of a new capitalism' and that 'traditional narratives of capitalism' should be reframed around its concepts (2010: 268).

attempt to theorise and justify a more ethical set of objectives for the corporation. On the other hand, they are explicit that their approach is still entirely consistent with the basic ethical framework of a market economy. This is clearly a challenge to libertarian defenders of the free market (Friedman, Sternberg, etc.) who think that the ethical framework of capitalism can support only the shareholder theory of the firm. Therefore, although stakeholder theory addresses the concerns of those who make a direct link between ethical scandals and profit maximisation, it rejects the assumption that the only long-term solution is a complete overhaul of the capitalist system. The importance of stakeholder theory is its attempt to demonstrate how corporations can pursue socially responsible objectives and abandon the traditional shareholder perspective, without requiring a fundamental change in the structure of a market economy.[11]

A critique of stakeholder theory: the methodology

Before the argument can progress, it is important to arrive at a clear conceptual structure for the stakeholder approach. This is especially so because of the analytical nature of the criticisms that will be made. A clear structure can be arrived at by making an abstraction of the various elements that are common to almost every description or justification of the theory. It has to be acknowledged that 'it is a mistake to see stakeholder theory as a specific theory with a single purpose. Researchers would do well to see stakeholder theory as a set of shared ideas that can serve a range of purposes...' (Freeman et al. 2010: 79). However, a definition is needed here as a criterion for what *counts* as a stakeholder theory and what does not, with the aim being to capture the minimal content that these ideas share. The attempts at defining the theory cited in the preceding suggest a form of conclusion that all writers under this approach either assume[12] or try to prove: that

---

[11] For the purposes of this book, 'capitalism' and 'market economy' refer simply to an economic system in which trade (or market exchange) is a permissible form of economic activity. This definition is consistent with the stakeholder literature; for example, Freeman et al. (2010: 267) understand capitalism in the sense of 'how markets work'. Chapter 4 expounds the implications of this definition.

[12] As with the 'instrumental' CSR theories mentioned earlier, not all stakeholder theories give an explicit account of what a corporation's purpose should be.

it is morally legitimate for a business corporation to use the assets which belong to it as a legal entity to pursue an objective which is not reducible to realising the interests of shareholders. It has also been seen that the framework of a market economy is accepted by proponents of the stakeholder approach. It follows that the form of conclusion given here must always be understood in the context of the basic institutions of a capitalist economy, and as the analysis unfolds, the importance of this criterion will become apparent.

This definition of stakeholder theory is of course incomplete, not least because it refers only to the *absence* of an overriding claim for shareholder interests, and does not specify any particular stakeholders (e.g., suppliers, employees, managers, creditors, governments, local communities). One would expect any variant of the theory to include some reference to the claims of these groups, though which groups have legitimate claims may not be a matter of consensus. The overview given here is what can be called a 'non-precisive' abstraction,[13] in which certain features are identified as essential to the theory without every detail being specified. Because the matter at hand is the conceptual coherence of stakeholder theory, it is sufficient to isolate certain essential features and examine their mutual compatibility, without all its elements being exhausted.

However, what is said here about the method of carrying out a conceptual analysis of stakeholder theory is incomplete without a consideration of the epistemological status of the theory. The aspect of the theory under examination is specifically its *ethical* claims about the proper objectives of business. Accordingly, an answer to the epistemological problem of what an ethical theory can lay claim to must be assumed before the analysis can be carried out.

First, it is clear that to analyse the logical structure of stakeholder theory's ethical claims is to assume that an ethical claim (or 'value judgement') can have a logical structure. As will be seen, this assumption can be distinguished from a methodology of logical positivism, which in other respects this analytical approach might resemble.

Some are more directly normative than others. However, the extent to which a stakeholder theory can be entirely 'instrumental' is a matter of debate, and is discussed in Chapter 2.

[13] Long (2006) gives an excellent account of the historical emergence of this form of abstraction from Aristotle and Aquinas, and how it differs from Platonic 'precisive' abstraction.

The question is whether ethical judgements have *cognitive* value and express anything *propositional*, which in turn raises the further question of whether an ethical statement can refer to anything *objective*.[14]

A distinction can be made between cognitivist and non-cognitivist understandings of ethical language. The former holds that when ethical language is used an objective property of the world is being described, in the light of which the utterance made can be either true or false. Darwall gives the following account:

> The thesis that ethical convictions admit of truth and falsity in this way is called cognitivism. Cognitivists believe that claims made with ethical language, and the states of mind we call ethical convictions or beliefs, have propositional or cognitive content, that these concerns admit of literal truth or falsity, and that ethical claims or convictions are correct or incorrect if, and only if, the propositions they assert are true or false, respectively. (Darwall 1998: 71)

On the other hand, a non-cognitivist approach denies that ethical language actually refers to anything that could be true or false, and holds it instead to be the statement of a subjective preference, or merely the expression of an attitude or desire. This is the position taken by many logical positivists, including Russell (1935) and Stevenson (1963). According to Darwall, non-cognitivism holds that 'no ethical facts exist of the sort that could make ethical claims true, but it denies that any ethical claims are strictly false either. Ethical claims are not "apt" for truth or falsity. They assert nothing propositional' (1998: 71).

For a non-cognitivist, moral argument consists entirely in persuading others to adopt a certain preference or attitude, while the cognitivist proceeds on the basis that one might arrange reasoning and evidence to demonstrate the 'truth' of one's ethical view. It is important to note that this distinction does not concern whether 'objective truth' about ethics can actually be acquired, but only whether this possibility is assumed in the ordinary language people use when expressing their moral convictions.

If the experience of ethical conviction is considered phenomenologically, then considerations arise which suggest that ethical language generally has a propositional use. If one hears on the news that a group

---

[14] The rest of this section draws heavily on Mansell (2010).

of children have been kidnapped and are being tortured in order to extract money from their parents, one's first reaction might well be moral outrage. Imagine we now hear a person being interviewed who is trying to justify the torture of the children in terms of the political agenda of the kidnappers. If after hearing and considering all the justifications, we still feel the same outrage as before, would we feel that compared to the kidnappers we had merely a difference in attitude, or as Darwall (1998: 18) puts it, '[our] respective convictions appear to vie for a space that, logically, no more than one can occupy?' Would we not feel the conviction of the kidnappers to be not merely different from ours, but also *incorrect*? As Darwall argues:

> It is not unusual to hear people say, in one moment, that ethics is no more than opinion, taste, or preference and then vehemently express, in the next moment, some strong ethical view. In the latter instance, it certainly *looks* as if they are committed to the correctness of their view. Surely it looks that way to their interlocutors. (Darwall 1998: 19)

It therefore seems that ethical convictions can generally be said to differ from the mere tastes or attitudes that people have. There does appear to be a role for argument and counter-argument, which suggests that ethical language carries a propositional weight which goes beyond what is entailed in stating an attitude or preference. R. M. Hare (1963: 53) outlines what he sees as 'three necessary ingredients' of moral argument which allow us to reject alternative propositions. These are (1) Facts; (2) Logic; and (3) Inclination. With regard to the second of these, he writes:

> When we are trying, in a concrete case, to decide what we ought to do, what we are looking for . . . is an action to which we can commit ourselves (prescriptivity) but which we are at the same time prepared to accept as exemplifying a principle of action to be prescribed for others in like circumstances (universalisability). If, when we consider some proposed action, we find that, when universalised, it yields prescriptions which we cannot accept, we reject this action as a solution to our moral problem – if we cannot universalize the prescription, it cannot become an "ought". (1963: 51)

What Hare identifies here is that there are mechanisms of reasoning which people ordinarily use to test the validity of their moral arguments. This lends weight to the notion that people aspire to *correctness* in their judgements, and feel that others who differ from them can be 'wrong'. It may be objected that even if we can trace a certain objectivism in the way people express their convictions, it by no means follows that there really exist objective ethical facts that can be known and which categorically bind us to a certain course of action. Mackie (1977: 79), for example, suggests that this can be explained by 'patterns of objectification' where people internalise socially conditioned demands and desires, which come to represent categorical imperatives in the imagination, whereas in fact they are only hypothetical.

This view may be correct. Even if we assume a cognitivist understanding of ethical conviction, it does not follow that people actually grasp subject-independent facts when they express their moral convictions. However, on this point, Thomas Nagel (1980) provides an intervention which is worth quoting at length. He argues that this scepticism regarding the possibility of objective facts is due to an inappropriate allocation of the burden of proof – where unless something can be *demonstrated* its existence is called into doubt. He writes:

No demonstration is necessary in order to allow us to *consider* the possibility of agent-neutral reasons: the possibility simply *occurs* to us once we take up an objective stance. And there is no mystery about how an individual could have a reason to want something independently of its relation to his particular interests or point of view, because beings like ourselves are not *limited* to the particular point of view that goes with their personal position inside the world. They are also ... *objective selves*: they cannot *help* forming an objective conception of the world with themselves in it; they cannot help trying to arrive at judgements of *value* from that standpoint. (1980: 120–1; emphases in original)

It follows that despite the difficulty of *proving* the existence of objective ethical values, the propensity to consider ethics from an *objective standpoint* is such that a denial of the existence of ethical facts would run counter to the way that people actually experience ethics.

There is of course a great deal more which has been said on the question of ethical objectivity. The intention here has been to suggest that a cognitivist understanding of ethics, which holds that ethical language carries with it an aspiration to objective truth, is consistent with how people experience ethics. Even if the question is left open of whether the existence of ethical 'facts' can be demonstrated, it seems that an experience of ethical conviction carries with it an aspiration to correctness of judgement from a standpoint independent of one's class, race, culture, etc. If cognitivism is an accurate description of the way that ethical claims are made, and the claims of stakeholder theory are no exception in this respect, then an analysis of the logical structure of stakeholder theory is justifiable on epistemological grounds.

A critique of stakeholder theory: the structure

An outline is now given of how this analysis of stakeholder theory is developed through the book. Chapter 2 gives a detailed introduction to stakeholder theory, tracing the historical emergence of the term 'stakeholder' in organization theory, the difference between the 'normative' and 'instrumental' versions of the theory, and the way that the normative approach itself divides into two separate branches. One of these is the argument for representation on the board of directors for stakeholders who hold incomplete contracts with management and have transaction-specific assets at risk (Freeman and Evan 1990, Blair 1995, Etzioni 1998). On examination this approach proves to be logically compatible with the shareholder theory, which leads to the other branch as a more satisfactory normative theory. Here we find many arguments that employ a version of the 'social contract' method[15] and call for managers to act upon the dictates of distributive justice,[16] often relying upon a use of Rawls's (1999) 'veil of ignorance' at the level of the firm.[17]

Having introduced the different normative approaches, Chapter 3 explores the philosophical ideas they draw upon, and considers the implications that follow. In particular, I focus on the use of a Rawlsian 'veil of ignorance' (perhaps the most common normative method

---

[15] See for example McNulty (1975), Freeman and Evan (1990), Donaldson and Dunfee (1994, 1995, 1999), Freeman (1994), Keeley (1995), Cragg (2002), Toenjes (2002) and Sacconi (2004, 2006).

[16] See Blair (1995), Donaldson and Preston (1995), McMahon (1995), Van Buren III (2001), Sacconi (2004, 2006) and Velamuri and Venkataraman (2005).

[17] See Freeman and Evan (1990), Boatright (1994), Freeman (1994) and Sacconi (2004, 2006).

used by stakeholder theorists) and set this in the context of Rawls's own work – one version of the so-called social contract tradition. These philosophical ideas are explored in detail to establish the demands that would be placed on any stakeholder theory drawing on this approach. The principles of 'distributive justice' and 'fairness' are also examined. The chapter sets out the theoretical conditions which the concept of the corporation would have to meet if the underlying ethical principles of stakeholder theory are to be applied.

Chapter 4 examines the implications of seeing the corporation purely as a commercial association whose purpose can be reached only through market exchange. If a network of market-based contracts underpins the corporation's existence, then with which ethical principles must its purpose be consistent? Through an analysis of the concept of trade, a minimal set of ethical principles are argued for, without which market exchange itself would be impermissible. I find that given the minimal ethical principles of a market economy, a corporation understood in this way cannot have an objective separate from the interests of its shareholders. It is for this reason that the next chapter explores whether a corporation should be seen as something *more* than a commercial entity. Chapter 5 examines one possibility for seeing the corporation as arising through a contract that cannot be reduced to a commercial purpose. Returning to the basic principles of the Rawlsian social contract (and its historical precedents) identified in Chapter 3, it can be asked whether a corporation represents a common purpose of all its stakeholders in the same way that a state represents the common interest of all its subjects in the social contract method. If this analogy holds then one could posit the existence of a unanimous interest of all stakeholders which would not simply be reducible to shareholder interests.

Having analysed the possibility of the realisation of stakeholder theory in a market economy, Chapter 6 examines the strengths and weaknesses of the alternative shareholder view. Two well-known critiques of stakeholder theory are presented, which can broadly be classified as 'consequentialist' (e.g., Jensen 2002) and 'deontological' (e.g., Friedman 1970). I argue that only the latter provides a consistent defence of the shareholder view. If, in contrast to stakeholder theory, the shareholder approach is found to be broadly consistent with the moral principles of a market economy, it can still be asked whether there are circumstances in which these principles give an incomplete account of what an individual in an organisation ought to do. The limits of the shareholder approach as a remedy for the problems of the stakeholder view are then explored.

2 | An introduction to stakeholder theory

This chapter elaborates a detailed account of stakeholder theory in its various forms. I begin by considering the etymology of the words 'stake' and 'stakeholder', and I note the association of these terms with having something placed *at risk*, and hence having a vested interest in the outcome of an event or the success of a system or organisation in which one has invested. A relatively recent development in the etymology of 'stakeholder' has been its use in the political vocabulary surrounding the rise to power of New Labour in 1997. The concept proclaimed here is that of a 'stakeholder economy', in which giving a 'stake' to every member of society is a device to foster social cohesion and to give everyone a sense of responsibility for society as a whole. In the field of organisation theory writers such as Phillips (2003: 33) have insisted on a clear separation between the application of the theory for the individual organisation and its use in a wider political context. However, if one examines the normative principles that underpin each of these approaches, an emphasis on fairness and distributive justice can be seen as common to both.

Stakeholder theory at the level of the business organisation has not always been applied in a normative manner, however. Instead, it has often been employed in an instrumental fashion, as a means for achieving the traditional performance objectives of corporate strategy. This is certainly the case in what is perhaps the landmark publication in the field of stakeholder theory, Edward Freeman's (1984) *Strategic Management: A Stakeholder Approach*. Whether an instrumental version of stakeholder theory is in fact possible without a normative element has been a point of disagreement among writers in the field, but the evidence suggests that the concept of stakeholder theory is not reducible to an enlightened view of corporate strategy, but implies a managerial responsibility to align the objectives of the corporation with the interests of stakeholders. Having identified the importance of the normative dimension of stakeholder theory, I move to an exposition of some of the normative arguments that have been developed. The aim here is to explicate these theories staying close to the words of those who defend them. Chapter 3 then elucidates the political philosophies on which these ideas are based.

The etymology of 'stake' and 'stakeholder'

The earliest known instance of the word 'stake' in the English language, according to the *Oxford English Dictionary*, occurs in AD 1205 and refers to a post to which persons were bound for execution by burning. The word appears to have been derived from the Old English word *stacum*, as used by Alfred the Great (*c.* 893), meaning simply a wooden stick with a pointed end for driving into the ground to mark a boundary or site, to secure an animal or support a plant, etc. (*Oxford English Dictionary Online* 2000). Sometimes in conjunction with the function of execution, this continues to be the sole common use of the word until the sixteenth century.

Until that time there is no direct connotation of having something 'at stake' in an organisation. However, around 1530, a new meaning arises from which the concept of a 'stakeholder' in an organisation appears ultimately to be derived. This use of the word is as a verb: 'to stake', which means to wager or hazard money on the outcome of a game or contest (ibid.). The context here is that of gambling, though whether this is connected to the earlier use of the word to refer to a pointed stick is uncertain. According to the *Oxford English Dictionary*, it is possible that the later use derives from the phrase *on the stake*, which could refer to a custom of placing on a 'stake' or post the object (such as an item of clothing) hazarded on the result of a game or contest. It is apparently more probable, however, that the word comes from the Middle Dutch *staken*, which means 'to fix' or 'to place'. Either way, by 1540 there is evidence of the word 'stake' being used as a noun, in the same context as the verb: a 'stake' being that sum of money or valuable commodity which is placed at hazard to be taken by the winner of the game. The term *sweepstakes* for multiple bets in horse racing appears to have originated from this usage (*Online Etymology Dictionary* 2001).

The present-day meaning of holding a stake in an organisation seems to be derived from these early uses. By the early seventeenth century, the word appears to have transcended its original context of gambling money or commodities and could be used to mean anything that was placed at hazard, for example, 'to stake one's reputation' on the favourable outcome of an event. The earliest recorded use of the term *stakeholder* (or 'Stake Holder') in 1708 was still in the context of gambling, however, and referred to one who holds the stakes of a wager – in this case a servant (*Oxford English Dictionary Online* 2000). Out of the notion of placing something 'at stake' or staking something of value, it seems to have become acceptable to speak generally of having a stake in a concern (not just in the sense of gambling), where one's interests are affected by a possible outcome. The OED cites an example from 1784 of having a stake in a friend's recovery from illness, and in 1821 the *Times* writes of 'stakeholders in one system of liberty, property, laws, morals, and national prosperity' (ibid.). This is the first example of 'stakeholder' being used outside the context of placing a wager, but it is not until 1941 in the *Journal of Political Economy* that any use of 'stakeholder' in reference to a specific organisation is found.

By 1963 an explicit academic discussion is under way concerning the place of stakeholders in business corporations, which is the immediate inspiration for the development of what is known today as 'stakeholder theory'. Interestingly, Freeman et al. (2010: 46) cite a personal conversation recorded in Giles Slinger's PhD thesis (1999) in which Marion Doscher, a staff writer and editor at the 'Theory and Practice of Planning' Group of the Stanford Research Institute, comments that the term 'stakeholder' is 'old Scottish' and refers to 'those who have a legitimate claim on something of value'. This quotation dates from late 1962.

However, before I turn to organisational applications of the concept, an alternative understanding in *political* discourse is worth reflecting upon. This is the notion of a 'stakeholder economy', which served to mark out the intellectual vision of the UK Labour Party (or 'New Labour', as it was called at the time) in its rise to power in the mid-1990s. Friedman and Miles (2006: 28) observe that references to stakeholders in the mass media '[were] stimulated in the UK when the term was associated with the "New" Labour Government of Tony Blair and their "Big Idea" of the Third Way . . . along with their use of the term in specific policies, such as stakeholder pensions'. Laplume et al. (2008: 1159) argue that Tony Blair's use of the language of stakeholder theory offered 'practitioner validation for what had remained until then an academic construct'. The basic idea is that if a greater number of people possess a stake in the *society* of a nation, then a greater sense of mutual purpose and national cohesion will emerge, as people identify their own success with that of society as a whole.

The earliest example of this idea is found in an article written by Will Hutton for the *Guardian* newspaper (31 October 1994). He writes: 'Instead of the winner-take-all economy and polity, the aim should be a stakeholder economy and polity in which all have an interest' (cited in *Oxford English Dictionary Online* 2004). In making sense of this, it should be noted that if 'stakeholder' were used in its original context of gambling, then it would be quite possible for a winner to 'take all' and yet for every participant to have an interest in the game's outcome. If having an interest is to be opposed to a 'winner-take-all' scenario, then it must be assumed that if more people had an interest (or a 'stake') in the game (or economy/polity), the winnings would be more equally distributed. So if a greater number of people participate then a greater number will receive the benefits of the game.

However, it is clear in Tony Blair's 'Singapore Speech' in 1996 (the year prior to Labour's General Election victory of May 1997) that there is more to his idea of stakeholder participation than the distribution of wealth. Blair (1996) speaks of 'a Stakeholder Economy in which opportunity is available to all, advancement is through merit and from which no group or class is set apart or excluded. This is the economic justification of social cohesion, for a fair and strong society'. He goes on to speak of 'One Nation politics' and 'a sharing of the possibility of power, wealth and opportunity' (ibid.). The argument he makes is that people who possess a 'stake' in society will feel more responsibility for society, and they will identify themselves with a common social good that all 'stakeholders' will perceive. He refers to 'the recognition of a mutual purpose for which we work together and in which we all benefit' (ibid.). The value of people possessing a stake in the success of society is that out of a mutual pooling of risk, a sense of mutual purpose emerges and feelings of social cohesion are created. Blair says: 'If people feel they have no stake in society, they feel little responsibility towards it, and little inclination to work for its success' (ibid.).

The original meaning of the term – to place something at risk (e.g., through a wager) – is still retained in the political context, but is perceived by Hutton and Blair as a device for engineering social cohesion and a 'national consensus', by ensuring that all are motivated to take a direct interest in the success of society as a whole. Hutton and Blair also perceive this device as working in the same way at the level of an individual firm. For Hutton (1997: 9), corporate governance should be reformed 'to reflect the various interests that converge on the firm – suppliers, workers and trade unions, banks, as well as shareholders and directors. This is the central idea of the stakeholder economy'. Under current corporate governance arrangements, by which he seems to refer to the shareholder model, 'a narrow view is taken of wider responsibilities to stakeholders' (1997: 11). Again, Blair expresses a similar view:[1]

> But it is surely time to assess how we shift the emphasis in corporate ethos – from the company being a mere vehicle for the capital market – to be traded, bought and sold as a commodity; towards a vision of the company as a community or partnership in which each employee has a stake, and where a company's responsibilities are more clearly delineated. (1996)

However, the argument here is not exactly the same as that which is applied to society overall. In advocating a stakeholder conception of 'society', the emphasis is on *giving* to people a stake in social prosperity so that they recognise a mutual responsibility for the overall benefits of society. Making the currently dispossessed into stakeholders of society is what Blair and Hutton prescribe. For an individual business corporation, however, the case is only coherent if put slightly differently. If to have a stake retains part of its original meaning – to place something at risk – it is not clear in what sense corporate stakeholders can be *created* out of existing workers, suppliers, shareholders, etc. The very fact that they have an investment at risk would seem to make them stakeholders already. In recognising the significance of this application of the term, a further aspect of the moral outlook of Blair (1996) and Hutton (1997) is brought to light. It is not merely a question of giving people the incentive to work for the common good by making them identify their stakeholding with the common lot, but of respecting the fact that *if* a person has a stake in society (or a firm), then there are certain terms of fair co-operation in accordance with which they must be treated. In the context of the business corporation, this amounts to ensuring that managers take into account the fact that

---

[1] This is despite Hutton's (1997: 15) insistence that crucial differences do exist between his conception of a stakeholder economy and that of Tony Blair.

certain groups of people (workers, suppliers, etc.) have something at stake in the corporation, and to developing this into a conception of the ethical firm.

While this may at first appear rather vague, the way in which stakeholder theorists in the area of business ethics have done exactly this will be discussed shortly. It will be seen that the same dual emphasis on recognising the stakes held by various investors in an organisation and the requirement to uphold certain ethical standards in respect of stakeholders, which underpins the idea of a 'stakeholder economy', is common also to stakeholder theories of the individual firm. Before engaging with these theories I first look at the initial development of the stakeholder concept in organisation theory, and the question of whether it can be used instrumentally as a tool for corporate strategy, or if it is an inherently normative concept which always implies a particular defence of corporate responsibility.

Stakeholder theory in organisations

There is some debate concerning the origin of the term 'stakeholder' in the management field. According to Freeman (1984: 31), the earliest use occurred in an internal memorandum at the Stanford Research Institute (now SRI International, Inc.), in 1963. The definition of 'stakeholder' given there was 'those groups without whose support the organisation would not exist' and the intention was to generalise beyond the notion of the shareholders being the only group to whom management need be responsive, because 'the continued survival of the firm' (1984: 32) could not be guaranteed without the support of these other groups. However, Freeman et al. (2010: 47) acknowledge the implications of Slinger's (1999) unpublished research into the history of the stakeholder concept: 'The original idea was not a matter of firm survival but rather a way to understand how a firm could meet the expectations of groups in its environment.' Slinger (1999: 46, cited in Freeman et al., 2010: 47) gives the original definition as follows:

Determination of corporate purpose requires comprehensive information about the expectations of the firm's 'stakeholders'. (These are all groups – such as owners, employees, and suppliers – who have something directly at stake in the company's progress.) (Stewart et al. 1963: 1)

Slinger (1999) connects this early development of the idea to the human relations approach at the Tavistock Institute in London, and finds that the appropriate foundational disciplines were psychoanalysis and social psychology, especially the theory of groups (Freeman et al. 2010: 47). On the other hand, Freeman et al. argue that the differences in the two definitions are 'a matter of degree' and that the focus on survival is 'appropriate for the more economic views of the firm that are influential in business today' (ibid.).

This latter understanding is the basis of what is in all probability the most cited definition of an organisational 'stakeholder': that given by Freeman (1984: 46).[2] His definition potentially encompasses a broader range of stakeholders than that provided by the SRI: 'A stakeholder in an organisation is (by definition) any group or individual who can affect or is affected by the achievement of an organisation's objectives'. Friedman and Miles (2006: 8) argue that compared with the SRI definition the concern with firm survival is here rather remote: 'there are many groups that are affected by the achievement of the organization's objectives, but that would not be thought of by anyone as having their support required for the organisation to exist'. However, Freeman's (1984) argument suggests that his definition is concerned above all with the long-term survival of a firm. He claims that it is necessary to consider not merely those who can affect the organisation, but also those who can be affected, because 'Groups which 20 years ago had no effect on the actions of the firm, can affect it today, largely because of the actions of the firm which ignored the effects on these groups. Thus, by calling those affected groups "stakeholders", the ensuing management model will be sensitive to future change' (1984: 46).

Freeman therefore argues that the survival of the business in the long run depends upon paying attention to those groups that could have an effect in the future as a result of being affected in the present. Freeman et al. (2010: 54) observe that the definition is developed from the viewpoint of the executive and addresses the need for an explicit strategy for dealing with stakeholders that can affect the firm. As Goodpaster (1991: 59) suggests, Freeman could have more clearly

---

[2] In a list of seventy-five texts published between 1963 and 2003 offering 'stakeholder' definitions, Friedman and Miles (2006: 4–8) find that Freeman's (1984) definition is by far the most popular, having been adopted by seventeen other texts.

defined a stakeholder as a group or individual who can 'actually or potentially affect' a business.

In considering whether Freeman's (1984) definition of a stakeholder can form part of a moral framework for business, what is immediately clear is that the role of a stakeholder in Freeman's thinking is instrumental, or a relevant factor for strategy, rather than having explicit implications for the moral responsibility of management. Other examples from Freeman's (1984) book serve to illustrate this point. He writes: 'My focus is on how executives can use the concept, framework, philosophy and processes of the stakeholder approach to manage their organisations more effectively' (1984: 27). Elsewhere he talks about 'developing the stakeholder concept into an approach to strategic management' (1984: 47), and furthermore he says that as the 'reason for being' of most organisations is to serve some need in their external environment: 'the more we can begin to think in terms of how to better serve stakeholders, the more likely we will be to survive and prosper over time' (1984: 80).

There is little in these comments to suggest that stakeholder theory, for Freeman (1984), concerns the problem of what is *morally* right for a business to do. It has often been suggested that Freeman's (1984: 46) definition of a stakeholder is inadequate because it could logically include a group of terrorists, but when one considers his definition purely in terms of strategy, there is nothing objectionable in this. As he explains:

Some groups may have as an objective simply to interfere with the smooth operations of our business. For instance, some corporations must count 'terrorist groups' as stakeholders. As unsavoury as it is to admit that such 'illegitimate' groups have a stake in our business, from the standpoint of strategic management, it must be done. Strategies must be put in place to deal with terrorists if they can substantially affect the operations of the business. (1984: 53)

However, I earlier considered the specification of moral legitimacy to be central to the idea of the stakeholder approach if it is viewed from a normative perspective. Freeman's strategic use of the theory can thus be considered *instrumental*, and lacking an explicit normative dimension. As a colleague of Freeman, Robert A. Phillips (1997: 53), has said of Freeman's (1984) work: 'The arguments are straightforwardly prudential in nature and seem to view stakeholders instrumentally'. However, it is not the case that Freeman believes that his strategic approach excludes the possibility of asking moral questions about corporate objectives. He certainly does not endorse here what he later describes as a mistaken 'separation thesis': the idea that business decisions have no moral content and moral decisions have no business content (Freeman 1994: 412). It just is not his intention here to provide a fully normative stakeholder theory. In considering the moral problems of stakeholder legitimacy, he writes: 'For the present time I shall put such questions aside, not because they do not bear fruitful research, but rather, I believe that first we must understand the weaker sense of "stakeholder legitimacy": if you want to be an effective manager, then you must take stakeholders into account' (1984: 45).

Freeman's strategic version of stakeholder theory therefore cannot be considered a moral justification for an alternative to shareholder theory. Stakeholders only have 'legitimate interests' to the extent that they have a bearing on management's ability to ensure the survival of the business, and it seems inconceivable that this would ever run contrary to the interests of shareholders. Freeman gives no argument in this work for the interests of stakeholders being ultimate objectives for a corporation to pursue, and given the strategic context in which it is written, his definition of a stakeholder is perfectly consistent with the shareholder theory of Milton Friedman (1970) and others.[3] As Phillips (1997: 53) remarks: 'Insofar as this "prudential stakeholder model" relies only on considerations of organisational well-being, it may be perfectly consistent with the claim that a manager's only obligation is to increase the profits of shareowners'. Despite the landmark status of Freeman's (1984) book in the history of stakeholder thought, it seems that one must look elsewhere for an alternative ethical argument to that of running the corporation directly in the interests of shareholders.

---

[3] Freeman et al. (2010: 11) in turn describe Friedman as an 'instrumental stakeholder theorist'. As discussed earlier, in terms of day-to-day management there is prima facie compatibility between the two perspectives. The theories differ on the ethical purpose of business and the question of whether managers are ultimately accountable to shareholders alone.

Ethics and strategy

The way that I have characterised the instrumental nature of Freeman's (1984) stakeholder theory appears to draw an unproblematic distinction between corporate strategy and ethics. However, the distinction between strategic and ethical ways of viewing the corporation is perhaps more problematic than I have suggested. Before an in-depth look at the ethical arguments given for a stakeholder alternative to the shareholder model, the question ought to be asked whether stakeholder theory can be inherently normative, instrumental or a combination of the two.

In recent years much scepticism has arisen regarding the authenticity of corporate codes of conduct, where a public display of ethical commitment by a corporation is taken to mask a deeper prudential concern with the bottom line and traditional performance objectives (Roberts, 2003; Jones et al., 2005). If stakeholder theory is assumed to be part of the canon of business ethics, then should it be merely a useful concept for management in improving the financial success of business, or can it set out a disinterested moral view? Jones et al. (2005: 123) take a straightforward view of the matter: 'the stakeholder approach to CSR retains a strategic element, in that the goals and objectives of the organisation are the central focus,[4] and stakeholders are a nuisance or opportunity that has to be managed'. Companies, they claim, 'distract or placate' stakeholders in order to continue with business as usual. This view is of course a highly cynical take on 'business as usual' which seems to assume that 'the goals and objectives of the corporation' are necessarily at odds with stakeholder interests. However, this would appear a good point to ask whether a tension between ethics and strategy has been acknowledged in the stakeholder literature, and if so, how advocates of a stakeholder approach have sought to reconcile the two.

[4] As the passage in which this sentence appears is a critique of how strategic concerns have to come to compromise the idea of responsibility held by corporations, the tautology in the first part of the sentence (if the objectives of a corporation are *not* its central focus, then what would be?) could only be explained by the prior assumption that a corporation's objective is necessarily to act for its shareholders – and hence not to exercise genuine responsibility. The implications of this assumption for Jones et al.'s (2005) argument are interesting but cannot be pursued further here.

Kaler (2002: 91) discusses recent literature that has surveyed different definitions of what it is to be a stakeholder, and concludes that
'there is a more or less even split between definitions which see stakeholders as people for whom businesses have to take responsibility and
definitions which see them as people who have to be taken account of
but not necessarily because of any responsibility for them'. This would
seem to suggest that there is a split between normative and instrumental approaches across the spectrum of stakeholder theory. However,
Kaler (2003: 92) argues, 'for the purposes of business ethics, some
form of claimant definition is required . . . the claim in question has to
be moral, and [what] it amounts to is the imposing of a requirement
upon businesses to serve the interests of their stakeholders'.

Kaler makes the seemingly justifiable point that business ethics is
by definition interested in asking what the objectives of a business
ought to be. It follows that any talk of stakeholders would have to
be concerned with the validity of their moral claims, to allow a normative assessment of what business ought to do with respect to them.
A discussion of stakeholders solely on the grounds of how they can
influence or affect the achievement of a company's objectives would
clearly be about strategy rather than ethics, because it would take the
organisational objectives as given and enquire only as to the best means
to achieve them, rather than the desirability of the ends themselves.
Kaler (2003: 81) argues for this reason that 'instrumental *stakeholder*
theory' is in fact an indirect approach to shareholder theory, as long
as it leaves it unchallenged that a corporation's objectives are those of
its shareholders.

Goodpaster (1991: 60), who draws a conclusion similar to that
of Kaler (2002, 2003), puts the issue succinctly: 'As an account of
how ethics enters the managerial mind set, the strategic stakeholder
approach fails not because it is *im*moral; but because it is *non* moral'
(emphasis in original). There is evident recognition in the stakeholder
literature that strategy and ethics are not one and the same, and that
any questions asked about the two refer to very different things. However, the issue is complicated by arguments which hold that the most
effective way for a business to meet its social objectives is to inter-
pret its own self-interest more broadly.[5] As Moir (2001: 17) has

---

[5] In an interview on the *Today* programme on 5 January 2006, David Cameron
(leader of the Conservative Party) declared, 'I think that many businesses in this

commented: 'Proponents of CSR claim that it is in the enlightened self-interest of business to undertake various forms of CSR. The forms of business benefit that might accrue would include enhanced reputation and greater employee loyalty and retention'. However, as Moir goes on to say: 'this leaves open the issue of whether those advocates of enlightened self-interest are motivated by the profit motive...and regard greater CSR as the manner in which to achieve maximisation of shareholder wealth, or whether there is an underlying moral or ethical imperative. This tension is evident in current attempts to address the nature of CSR' (ibid.). This opens up the interesting question of whether the actions of a business can be said to be meeting the moral claims of stakeholders when those actions have desirable consequences for stakeholders, but the intention is only to respond to shareholders.[6]

One might assume that if a moral intention to act in accordance with stakeholder interests is essential for a stakeholder theory distinguishable from the shareholder approach, then a demarcation between a normative theory and one that is strategic or instrumental should be clear. However, Donaldson and Preston (1995) argue that in reality the normative version inescapably underpins any other version, and stakeholder theorists of all descriptions cling to a stakeholder approach only so long as they believe in its normative validity. Donaldson and Preston (1995) argue specifically that stakeholder theory falls into three categories: instrumental, normative and descriptive. The first two have already been touched upon. The descriptive version is based on the belief that regardless of what managers *ought* to do, or what would actually happen if they took stakeholders into account, managers nonetheless *believe* that the interests of stakeholders should be pursued. The descriptive version is simply an empirical claim about managerial beliefs, but Donaldson and Preston reason that

country want to do more in terms of helping with our social problems...and they know it's not just good for altruistic reasons, it's also good for them and I want to encourage that kind of spirit in business' (British Broadcasting Corporation 2006). What Cameron does not say here is whether a business would be obliged (morally or legally) to help with social problems, even if it could *not* justify such a course of action to its shareholders.

[6] Graafland et al. (2004: 141) explain that one of the biggest barriers to the effective benchmarking of corporate social responsibility is the gap between intentions and consequences, which cannot be observed empirically.

By the logic of descriptive justification, if new surveys showed that managers were abandoning stakeholder orientations... the theory would be invalidated. But this observation offers a significant clue about the nature of the theory itself, because few if any of its adherents would be likely to abandon it, even if current legal or managerial trends were to shift. (1995: 77)

According to them, the same can also be said of the instrumental version. Although many supporters of this version are keen to cite its consistency with traditional performance objectives, 'few of them would abandon the concept if it turned out to be *equally* efficacious as other conceptions' (1995: 81). The point here is that if managerial attitudes to CSR and stakeholders became neutral, and an emphasis upon serving stakeholder needs did *not* lead to successful corporate performance, few supporters of stakeholder theory on descriptive or instrumental grounds would drop the approach altogether. This suggests that the very concept of 'stakeholder' in an organisational context is largely meaningless if it is not underpinned by normative concerns, however implicit these are.[7] If Donaldson and Preston's assessment of opinion in the field until 1995 is accurate, much of the cynicism with which stakeholder theory is regarded appears to be misplaced. Stakeholder theory as an idea cannot simply be reduced to a self-interested concern with strategy and marketing, as Jones et al. (2005: 123) would have it.

Jones and Wicks (1999) argue that even if one could separate the instrumental and normative approaches, it makes sense from a normative approach to attempt a *convergence* with instrumental considerations. The assumed compatibility between stakeholder theory and business in a capitalist system is at the core of Jones and Wicks's (1999) argument: they see the need to ground questions of business ethics in a practicable framework that accommodates the profit motive. The issue at stake for all stakeholders is the survival of the business, because

whatever the interests of core stakeholders in the firm – groups that invest in the firm and help make it a going concern... they also have an interest in it staying in business. That is the only way these stakeholders can get

---

[7] Freeman (1999: 234), in rejecting the usefulness of Donaldson and Preston's descriptive–instrumental–normative typology, writes, '*Stakeholder* is an obvious literary device meant to call into question the emphasis on "stockholders". The very idea of a purely descriptive, value-free, or value-neutral stakeholder theory is a contradiction in terms' (emphasis in original).

their benefits from the firm over time. This means that there is a normative basis – grounded in the legitimate interests of core stakeholders – for the firm to also focus on the instrumental aspects of its operations (i.e., making a profit). (1999: 621–2)

This is what Jones and Wicks (1999) call 'Convergent Stakeholder Theory', which suggests that for shareholder and stakeholder interests to be met, both need to be pursued in tandem. As Donaldson (1999: 240) has pointed out, if management believe that they *ought* to be pursuing the legitimate interests of stakeholders, they must believe that this will be consistent with the long-term survival of the company, so that these interests *can* ultimately be fulfilled. Donaldson (1999: 240) reasons that under competitive conditions, a managerial objective that is not instrumentally optimal for the company's performance would become untenable, and so there must be compatibility between the normative and instrumental approaches.[8]

As discussed above, Freeman maintains that any effective business strategy has to take into account the interests of stakeholders. Moreover, in recent years, his argument has been that this is intrinsically a moral endeavour: creating value for stakeholders *means* paying attention to questions of ethics. As Freeman et al. put it:

To create value for stakeholders, executives must understand that business is fully situated in the realm of humanity. Businesses are human institutions populated by real live complex human beings. Stakeholders have names and faces and children. They are not mere placeholders for social roles. As such, matters of ethics are routine when one takes a 'managing for stakeholders' approach. (2010: 29)

Furthermore, Freeman et al. (2010: 6) employ a version of G. E. Moore's 'open question' argument to establish that, for any theory which may explain a business decision, 'ethical questions are always there'. They argue that it is possible to ask with regard to almost any business decision who is harmed and/or benefited, for whom value is created and destroyed, whose rights are enabled and whose values are realised (2010: 7). A related argument is that one cannot entirely isolate

---

[8] Mitchell (1986) discusses how a corporation's capacity for social policy is proportional to the lack of competitiveness in its market, and if competition increases then opportunities for pursing 'social' ends will tend to diminish.

a factual statement (e.g., that a particular strategy will create economic value for shareholders) from its moral context and implications. Harris and Freeman (2008) draw upon the pragmatist philosophy of Quine, Dewey and Rorty to argue that values and statements of fact are necessarily 'entangled' and 'interconnected'.[9] All economic considerations therefore have ethical values 'lurking beneath the surface' (Harris and Freeman 2008: 542–3).

So it can be seen that, contrary to the criticism that the ethical approach of stakeholder theory is inauthentic and concerned only with strategy, there is a genuine recognition of the need to separate moral responsibility to stakeholders from a purely instrumental and amoral approach that seeks only to reward shareholders. Freeman and his pragmatist co-authors clearly regard the latter as an incoherent idea in the first place. There is of course a concern with strategy to the extent that actions taken by management must be viable for the survival of the business in the long run. If this were not so, then a normative purpose of creating value for all stakeholders groups could not be sustained.

However, the fact that every stakeholder theory assumes a normative position does not tell us how all stakeholders, including shareholders, could have morally legitimate interests that should be pursued simultaneously. If normativity and instrumentality are intertwined, then are shareholders' interests to be satisfied only because stakeholder objectives are thereby fulfilled? Is managerial responsibility to shareholders then contingent upon stakeholder interests? Jones and Wicks (1999: 622–3) claim that the interests of all (legitimate) stakeholders have intrinsic value, but that they should *not* be weighted equally. However, they do not provide any explanation for how such claims *could* be weighted.

Given that different stakeholders are likely to have different interests over time, and not all these interests can be treated equally at all times, there is a need for a normative theory to provide some indication about *which* interests should be given priority over others and

---

[9] The use of such terms implies that for these stakeholder theorists 'facts' and 'values' are not literally identical. In other words, not every factual statement is a statement *about* value. It should therefore be possible to distinguish stakeholder theories with an ethical focus from those that assume a moral position without arguing for it explicitly. 'Instrumental' stakeholder theories would be examples of the latter.

why.[10] If shareholder interests are subordinated to the needs of other legitimate stakeholders, an idea at the core of stakeholder theory, then a moral position will have to be justified that ascribes legitimacy to non-shareholder interests equal to (or greater than) those of shareholders. To this end, I will outline a range of defences for a normative stakeholder approach, and explore whether there is a common set of ethical principles to be found in the arguments made.

Normative arguments for stakeholder theory

The normative arguments for stakeholder theory can be divided into two categories. One category is opposed to corporate governance arrangements in which only shareholders possess certain rights with respect to corporate control, such as the right to elect directors or to vote on changes to the articles of association, dividends, etc. Instead it is argued that other stakeholders such as employees and consumers face a greater risk by virtue of their particular investments in a company than do shareholders, and hence have a greater entitlement to exercise 'control' over the corporation – for example, through voting membership on the board of directors. It is claimed therefore that a model of governance in which the corporation is run for the sole interest of shareholders is not tenable. In the second category, it is argued that the fair terms on which all stakeholders would choose to interact with each other would not countenance an organisation run for the sole benefit of one stakeholder (i.e., the shareholders), but instead that the interests of *all* stakeholders must be encompassed in the organisation's objectives. Stated simply, these are the two lines of argument used to defend a normative stakeholder theory of the firm. For reasons which will emerge, the second argument is far more persuasive and significant as a moral alternative to the shareholder view. However, I begin with an examination of the first category.

As will be shown in Chapter 4, stakeholder theorists commonly assume a *contractual* theory of the firm. Whatever else an organisation might possess by way of attributes, the modern business corporation is seen as a network of contracts entered into by a range of

---

[10] It is the contention of Freeman et al. (2010) that to create value a business should minimise trade-offs between stakeholders, and certainly should not prioritise stakeholders. I will try to establish in Chapter 5 why Freeman et al.'s (2010) perspective is in fact compatible with the argument set out in this book.

investors (employees, suppliers, lenders, managers, shareholders, etc.), each expecting to make an economic gain. The argument has been made by Oliver Williamson (1985) that in most circumstances only the shareholders should be given voting membership on the board of directors, because only they face a firm-specific risk without safeguards to prevent their entire investment from being expropriated. The shareholders therefore face a unique *residual* risk, and their only safeguard is to exercise ultimate control over the board. The institution of the board arises endogenously, as 'a governance structure that holders of equity recognise as a safeguard against expropriation and egregious mismanagement' (1985: 305). Only shareholders are entitled to exercise control in this way, because other investors are better able to develop safeguards to protect the risk of their investments. As an example of such a safeguard, Williamson (1985: 303–4) agrees with the idea of board representation for workers for informational purposes, which 'can be especially important during periods of actual or alleged adversity' (1985: 303), but not for direct control. He also points to how short-term lenders are protected by the proof that a firm is financially sound, and long-term lenders can place preemptive claims against durable assets, so that neither need the additional protections given to shareholders (1985: 307). There is more complexity to the framework of his argument than it has been possible to cover here, but these are the basic points that have attracted the attention of stakeholder theorists.

Freeman and Evan (1990) and Blair (1995) build on Williamson's (1985) argument that it is economically efficient for contractors to agree to safeguards that protect the transaction-specific nature of their investments, but disagree that shareholders are the only investors entitled to a privileged position in corporate governance (e.g., voting membership on the board). Freeman and Evan (1990: 349) argue that 'it would be irrational for stakeholders to give up the ability to participate in monitoring the actual effects of the firm on them, and therefore the right to make changes in the contractual mechanism'. They conclude that 'it is rational for stakeholders to choose voting membership on the board, in addition to whatever other safeguards may be feasible' (ibid.). Blair (1995: 231) argues that the limited liability of shareholders necessarily means that other investors face a risk that cannot be mitigated by contractual safeguards. In other words, they face a 'residual' risk, and 'if other stakeholders could be shown to share in the residual gains and risks, their interests in being able to exercise some control over corporations would be significantly legitimised'. She focuses in particular on employees who have developed firm-specific human capital and should therefore have the same monitoring rights as shareholders to protect their investment. Likewise, Etzioni (1998: 683), in a communitarian defence of stakeholder theory, writes that as the return on any stakeholder's investment is not guaranteed, 'all are entitled to form a relationship with the users of their resources to help ensure that the usage will be in line with their interests and values'.

Although this discussion about the rights of firm-specific investors to participate in corporate decision making is invoked to support a normative stakeholder view of the firm, the logic of the connection is not obvious. Whatever the merits of this discussion, it seems to apply only to the feasibility of governance arrangements in protecting the substance of contracts entered into by stakeholders. It says nothing about the substance of these contracts or the objectives that a corporation can pursue legitimately. The arguments of these writers are plausible as regards the identification of residual risk in investments made by non-shareowning investors and the suggestion that they might be entitled to protection normally enjoyed only by shareholders. However, their arguments do not justify the moral desirability of one corporate objective over another. Their suggestions could be useful remedies for 'contractual incompleteness' and the residual risk that affects non-shareowning investors, but their position does not rule out the shareholder wealth-maximising objective: it merely adds to the constraints that management might be obliged to observe in its pursuit.

Marcoux (2003: 24) expresses this position clearly when he addresses the view of Blair (1995) and others that 'employees and suppliers make asset-specific investments in the firm, and . . . this constitutes a vulnerability that justifies a claim to management in behalf of their interests', and asks: 'why does this legitimate vulnerability give rise to claims that firms be managed in employees' and suppliers' behalf? Why does it not merely give rise to certain threshold claims on the firm, e.g. to notice and/or severance before closing a plant or terminating a supply arrangement?' (ibid.) In other words, the rights of these vulnerable investors could be seen as constraints on the maximisation of shareholder value, but not as a substitute for it. For this, an explicit set of ethical principles would need to be defended that, when applied to the firm, point to a *different* objective.

The remaining normative arguments for stakeholder theory are those which provide an ethical theory of the corporate objective which is irreducible to pursuing the interests of shareholders.[11] The ethical principles employed can be classified into four groups.[12] First there are writers who have tried to identify the fair terms on which all stakeholders of a corporation would voluntarily co-operate with each other for mutual advantage. In other words, on what grounds can we assume that the entity that is a corporation is the result of the voluntary consent of all those who interact with it (the corporation being understood here as a network of contracts)? A similarity can be seen to the political concept of stakeholding, which draws a connection between stakeholding and a fair distribution of the wealth of society. The contractual method and the two 'principles of justice' proposed by Rawls in his *A Theory of Justice* (1999) are applied by stakeholder theorists to the individual corporation and form the moral basis of this perspective. A smaller group of theories can be found in which the focus is not so much on identifying the moral principles that should govern the internal constitution of a corporation, but on attributing responsibility for carrying out the broader goals of society to the corporation. The implication, though this is not often clearly articulated, is that individual business corporations should be given the executive power of civil society, with a mandate by the state (or the sovereign power) for realising the 'public interest'.

Conversely, Robert Phillips (2003) argues that a corporation is fundamentally different from a state, and comparisons are useless for deriving a corporation's moral objectives. Instead, he focuses on the principle of *fairness* (like most other stakeholder theorists, taking Rawls as his inspiration). An approach similar to that of Phillips, and again inspired by Rawls, is to use the concept of *distributive justice* to place qualifications on the property rights of shareholders, and hence to advance a stakeholder theory of the firm. This differs from the first group in that the concept of distributive justice as applied to the firm is not defended by a contractual method: instead it is applied directly. These four areas are now elucidated in turn.

---

[11] This characterisation accords with the abstract definition of stakeholder theory set out in Chapter 1.

[12] There may be ethical principles falling outside this classification that could in theory support a normative stakeholder approach. However, the analysis here is limited to those principles that have in fact been employed in the writings of stakeholder theorists.

Perhaps the first attempt to use a contractual method to offer a solution to the question of a corporation's objective was that of Freeman and Evan (1990). As explained earlier, their main purpose is to use Williamson's (1985) transaction cost approach to go beyond Williamson's own conclusions, by arguing for board representation as a safeguard for the contractual rights of non-shareholding stakeholders. One part of their argument is that if transaction costs are a natural part of any contract, then 'All parties to a contract, if a modicum of efficiency is to be preserved . . . must have a right to bargain' (1990: 348). How they establish this right to bargain need not be discussed here; what is more important is the implication they draw from this:

> If all parties that are affected by a contract have a right to bargain about the distribution of those effects, then we naturally ask, 'what is rational for each party to accept in the way of constraints?' A minimal condition would be a notion of 'fair contract', whereby governance rules could be devised to ensure that the interests of all parties are at least taken into consideration. (Ibid.)

This raises the further question of how to establish criteria for a 'fair' contract; Freeman and Evan (1990) answer that a readily applicable device for establishing fairness is the Rawlsian 'veil of ignorance' (ibid.). Just as Rawls (1999) held that the principles of justice for regulating the basic social institutions would be those chosen by people in ignorance of their actual place in society, Freeman and Evan (1990: 349) write that stakeholders who make up a corporation 'are to decide on these rules "behind a veil of ignorance", interpreted to mean, that no one knows which particular stake he or she actually holds in the corporation'.[13] Whatever procedures for bargaining between stakeholders would be chosen with this method would give rise to a 'fair contract'.

Freeman and Evan (1990) surmise that stakeholders would not give up the right to participate in monitoring the effects of the firm on them, so they must have the right to voting membership on the board, even if they may not exercise this right in practice because of the costs of

---

[13] While my aim at this stage is primarily to represent the *intentions* of these authors, questions can of course be asked about their interpretation of philosophical sources. Child and Marcoux (1999) make excellent criticisms of the use of Rawls's 'veil of ignorance' by Freeman and Evan (1990) and Freeman (1994) in supporting stakeholder representation on a board of directors.

doing so. Freeman and Evan do not expand beyond this point in this article, and as I argued above, for stakeholders to have a right to board participation as a safeguard for their contractual rights does not necessarily contradict the shareholder view. However, the importance of Freeman and Evan's (1990) argument is their introduction of a *method* that could be used in principle to establish corporate obligations that go beyond shareholder wealth. This is inherent in the passage cited above, in which the rules of a fair contract are established as constraints on the right to bargain 'about the distribution of those effects' (1990: 348). If by the 'effects' of the contracts entered into is meant simply the wealth generated by the corporation, then imposing a set of bargaining constraints that are hypothetically acceptable to all stakeholders would entail a corporate objective irreducible to shareholder interests.

A more developed use of Rawls's 'veil of ignorance' occurs in Freeman (1994). His argument begins by emphasising that with respect to the firm all stakeholders have equal moral rights, and there are no grounds for giving moral preference to one stakeholder over another. This mirrors Rawls's (1999) view that in society all people are regarded as having equal basic liberties. Freeman propounds 'the presumption of equality among the contractors, rather than the presumption in favour of financier rights' (1994: 415) and argues for 'a basic equality among stakeholders in terms of their moral rights as these are realised in the firm' (ibid.). Freeman then asserts that the firm can be seen as a contractual process among the parties affected, with all stakeholders being free to create value for themselves, and he goes on to ask under what conditions this contract would be *fair*. Following Rawls, he writes that 'a contract is fair if parties to the contract would agree to it in ignorance of their actual stakes' (1994: 416) and asks us to imagine stakeholders situated behind a 'veil of ignorance', with no stakeholders knowing what particular stake they have in the corporation.

He argues that in this original position stakeholders would agree that 'inequalities among stakeholders are justified if they raise the level of the least well-off stakeholder'[14] (1994: 415–16), and in addition that a 'Doctrine of Fair Contracts' would emerge to provide the ground rules to guide stakeholders in devising a 'corporate constitution or charter'

---

[14] This mirrors Rawls's (1999) 'Difference Principle'. His principles of justice and arguments for them are discussed in Chapter 3.

(1994: 417). Freeman (1994: 416–17) argues that the ground rules agreed upon by all stakeholders would include a 'Principle of Governance' where there must be unanimous consent among stakeholders for changing 'the rules of the game' (which might include the articles of the corporation – usually a shareholder voting matter), and 'The Agency Principle', stipulating that any agent must serve the interests of all stakeholders. A total of six ground rules – covering externalities, contracting costs, terms of entry and exit, etc. – are given, and on this basis Freeman wishes to reform corporation law. One consequence is that 'Corporations shall be managed in the interests of its stakeholders, defined as employees, financiers, customers, employers, and communities'[15] (1994: 417). It clearly follows that the objective of the corporation under Freeman's (1994) theory cannot be reduced to shareholder interests, and this seems a natural implication of including the interests of *all* stakeholders in the hypothetical contract which establishes the ground rules for a 'corporate constitution'.

A final example of the Rawlsian method being applied in stakeholder theory is the work of Sacconi (2004, 2006), who makes an extensive and sophisticated application of Rawls's theory to the problems of corporate governance and accountability. Sacconi (2004) sees CSR as an extended form of governance to remedy the incomplete nature of corporate contracts. He argues that management must have a fiduciary duty to non-controlling stakeholders (which includes any stakeholders 'locked in' by their firm-specific investments; Sacconi 2004: 7) to ensure that no stakeholders are deprived of their fair share of the surplus produced by the corporation. The question is: what is to count as a 'fair' share? In common with Freeman (1994), Sacconi (2004) envisages a hypothetical 'social contract' generating impartially acceptable agreements. He gives a list of rules (2004: 13) which should govern the bargaining process behind the 'veil of ignorance'. These include the setting aside of force, fraud and manipulation; the necessity of cooperation by all stakeholders after each has put himself in the position of the others; and the insistence that agreements must be willingly accepted by all stakeholders. On this basis stakeholders are assumed to come

---

[15] The definition of a stakeholder has undergone a change here from his (1984: 46) definition: 'any group or individual who can affect or is affected by the achievement of an organisation's objectives'. No reason is given here for this change in definition.

together to reach a 'first social contract', in which they would agree to produce the maximum surplus possible and distribute this surplus in a way that is rationally acceptable to each stakeholder (2004: 14–15). In this way 'fairness' of distribution is guaranteed.

A distinctive element in Sacconi's model is that stakeholders are assumed to reach this first social contract prior to the employment of management: 'After comparative examination of the governance costs of each stakeholder, the one with the lowest costs is selected and assigned ownership' (2004: 15), and this occurs *after* the first social contract is reached, under a 'second social contract'. Management is then employed to maximise the residual value of the firm. Therefore, Sacconi challenges the view that shareholders are the single group who employ management. Under this 'second social contract', management must 'remunerate the owners with the maximum residual compatible with fair remuneration – as defined by the first social contract' (2004: 16), and other stakeholders should also be remunerated in accordance with this contract (ibid.). In a later paper, Sacconi (2006: 268) writes of this first contract as a 'constitutional choice' which must be made 'unanimously' by all potential members of the association. Further-more, 'the only rational agreement is the one that involves all the members', because if this unanimous agreement is not reached then the constitution cannot be established and all stakeholders are condemned to a 'State of Nature' outside the corporation (ibid.). It follows that the rational bargaining here is *impartial* and the results will not neces-sarily reflect the interests of any particular individual. He writes: 'not only do all the parties *rationally* accept the solution (which is therefore equally rational for them all) but the solution is anonymous' (2006: 269, emphasis in original).

Other applications of Rawls's theory of distributive justice can be found in the work of Jackson (1993), Burton and Dunn (1996) and Velamuri and Venkataraman (2005). The assumption that the cor-poration can be seen as a voluntary association of all stakeholders, in the context of which it can be asked what the 'fair' terms of this association might be, is central to these approaches.

A second line of argument holds that instead of being run in the interests of shareholders, business corporations should have as their objective at all times the 'public interest'. Clearly, it is one thing to say that the laws of a country are passed by the legislature with the public interest in mind, and when a business observes them it would in effect be acting in a way compatible with the public interest. It is quite another to assert that the public interest should serve as the defining purpose of the corporation and *replace* (rather than constrain) traditional corporate objectives. This latter position is implicit in the argument of Boatright (1994), who writes that the accountability of managers to shareholders should be maintained in law only on grounds of public policy (1994: 400–3), and that the only 'contract' which binds managers is not with shareholders, but is a 'Rawlsian hypothetical contract' in which 'the whole of society' is involved (1994: 398). Kaler (2006: 253) makes a more explicit move in this direction. He argues against the property rights defence of shareholder theory as follows: 'even supposing that shareholders do own companies, there is clearly something decidedly indirect and restricted about their ownership that makes it not [at] all like the ownership of material possessions such as cars and houses'. He writes:

Property rights are far from absolute and frequently qualified or overridden by what are seen as more important moral considerations. When they are, this is sometimes a question of counterbalancing or conceding preference to a competing right to security and safety for instance . . . we routinely permit such considerations to override rights to such generalised prized possessions as land and buildings (even, it must be said, people's homes) when we require them to be sold in order for construction developments seen as being in the public interest to take place. (2006: 254)

Kaler goes on to ask why the property rights of shareholders in companies should not be subject to the same overriding considerations of the public interest. A further example of this approach is found in McNulty (1975). Though not calling her theory a stakeholder approach, she argues that governments have delegated responsibility for the public interest (following Rousseau, she calls this the 'general will') to corporations in the specific area of producing goods and services, and in return corporations have the right to make profits (1975: 582).

A focus on the public interest is also central to Scherer and Palazzo's (2007, 2011) 'political' conception of corporate responsibility. Acknowledging the 'new political role' of business in the provision of market regulation and public services that would previously have been guaranteed by nation-states, they ask what could establish the democratic legitimacy of this activity. They draw on Habermas's conception of deliberative democracy, in which legitimacy emerges from a proactive political engagement with 'civil society associations and movements that map, filter, amplify, bundle, and transmit private problems, needs and values'[16] (2007: 1107). They claim that business, especially in the form of multi-national corporations, should be fully embedded in deliberative processes of 'democratic will formation'. Scherer and Palazzo add that these processes, 'driven by civil society actors and spanning a broad field of public arenas, establish a *democratic control on the public use of corporate power*' (2007: 1109, emphasis in original). The aim is to 'domesticate economic pressures by democratic control' in a way that accepts a legitimate political role for the corporation (2007: 1097–8). The priority of the public interest for the corporate objective in this perspective is especially clear: 'the deliberative approach to CSR demands that the routine of corporate decision-making be cancelled by a public discourse on the legitimacy of a given issue' (2007: 1112).

For Scherer and Palazzo (2011), the political conception of CSR is particularly relevant for the case of weak or failed states that lack the power to enforce market regulation. This is most evident in the regulation of transnational economic forces:

On the global level, neither nation-states nor international institutions alone are able to sufficiently regulate the global economy and to provide global public goods. . . . [17] Unlike national governance with its monopoly on the use of force and the capacity to enforce regulations upon private actors within the national territory, global governance rests on voluntary contributions and weak or even absent enforcement mechanisms. (Scherer and Palazzo 2011: 900)

Business corporations, along with civil society groups, have a democratic responsibility to fill the gap: 'In a nutshell, political CSR suggests an extended model of governance with business firms contributing to global regulation and providing public goods' (2011: 901).[18]

---

[16] Weale (2007: 77–100) provides a useful critique of Habermas's argument and a comparison with other theories of deliberative democracy.

[17] Crane et al. (2008: 67–9) offer some illuminating examples.

[18] I have passed over these arguments rather quickly because a full analysis of the authors' normative framework would require investigating their empirical premise that failed or weak states provide the dominant regulatory context for corporate activity. This is beyond the scope of the current book. However, it is

The similarity in how these two branches of argument oppose the shareholder view is that both see the corporation as a voluntary association of many different stakeholder groups which all must have their interests considered, rather than just the shareholders. The difference is that the second group extends the relevant stakeholders to include all of society, which means that the corporation must simply represent the 'public interest', whereas the first group of authors would probably not extend the interests of the corporation this far.

An influential argument of a different form is that of Donaldson and Preston (1995), who focus on the link between property rights and distributive justice. They argue that 'stakeholder theory can be normatively based on the evolving theory of property' (1995: 83) and acknowledge a subtle irony in using property rights to justify the stakeholder view, as this justification is more commonly associated with the shareholder theory (e.g., Friedman 1970). To do this, they draw attention to the fact that property rights do not give the owners an unlimited right to do with their property as they will. Property rights, they argue, are part of human rights, and thus there are always limitations on what property owners can do as regards non-owners. They write: 'the contemporary theoretical concept of private property clearly does not ascribe unlimited rights to owners and hence does not support the popular claim that the responsibility of managers is to act solely as agents for the shareholders' (1995: 83–4).

However, this claim based on property rights is not incompatible with the moral principles underpinning the shareholder theory. As soon as one recognises that not just shareholders have property rights but rights of this kind are possessed by everyone else, then everyone's rights must be respected and cannot be overridden by one particular group. Nowhere in Friedman's (1962, 1970) liberal political theory is it stated that one particular group in society should be given exclusive rights that override the rights of all others. John Locke (1689/1988), in many ways an obligatory reference point for modern liberal defences of property,[19] advocates both a natural right of property and the equality

worth noting for present purposes that Scherer and Palazzo explicitly distance their argument from normative stakeholder theory (2007: 1111; 2011: 905) though it clearly fits my definition in Chapter 1.

[19] For example, Nozick (1974), Becker (1977) and Rothbard (1982).

of all citizens before the rule of law. Merely drawing attention to the fact that shareholders cannot use their property to violate the rights of others does not refute the shareholder view but may actually reinforce it. If indeed shareholders do have property rights, then perhaps these cannot be overridden by other stakeholders in the name of 'distributive justice', the 'public interest', or whatever else.

A more plausible challenge by Donaldson and Preston (1995) involves the question of distributive justice as the *source* of property rights. They write: 'Unless property rights are regarded as simple, self-evident moral conceptions, they must be based on more fundamental ideas of distributive justice' (1995: 84). This appeal to distributive justice, they believe, undermines the view that shareholders have exclusive property rights to a company's assets. They state: 'All critical characteristics underlying the classic theories of distributive justice are present among the stakeholders of a corporation' (ibid.). These characteristics, which they claim are the most relevant in determining a fair distribution of wealth and income, are 'need, ability, effort, and mutual agreement' (ibid.). They proceed to identify each of these characteristics with a group of stakeholders connected with a business. Their argument that property rights are constrained by distributive justice is accepted by Margaret Blair (1995: 224–5), in her stakeholder conception of corporate governance, as evidence for denying that shareholders own corporations.

A final principle employed as a defence of a normative stakeholder theory is the 'principle of fairness' articulated by Robert Phillips (1997, 2003), himself a former student of Freeman. Rejecting the notion of Freeman and others that a Rawlsian social contract theory can be applied to the corporation as if it were a state, Phillips instead argues that obligations to stakeholders should be based on a principle of fairness that applies in all voluntary associations set up for the mutual benefit of their participants. The key to his argument is that if the benefits of a cooperative scheme are accepted voluntarily, then obligations are incumbent upon all members of the scheme in proportion to the benefits they receive (2003: 91–2). It follows that an organisation incurs obligations to stakeholders in proportion to the benefits it receives from them. He adds that such obligations need not be created solely through consent: 'The voluntary engagement in, and acceptance of the benefits of, a cooperative scheme can similarly serve to create obligations.... Further, obligations of fairness exist even if the obligation creating implications of such activities are unknown to the actor' (2003: 91). Because many contracts formed with stakeholders are incomplete[20] and gaps are left undetermined by the legal system, the moral obligations of fairness appeal to the discretion of managers and 'add richness and detail to the thin, formal relationships established in contracts and other legislation' (2003: 93).

This is the role that Phillips sees for the 'principle of fairness' in establishing obligations to stakeholders. A vital question, however, concerns the entity that is supposed to incur 'obligations' to stakeholders and *what* is to count as a benefit. It is clear that for Phillips (2003) the entity under consideration is the organisation itself, which because of the contributions it receives from stakeholders incurs proportionate obligations to them. Phillips (2003: 92) remarks that 'organizations with commercial purposes and other private associations typically rely on merit or contribution as the appropriate scheme of distribution' and his principle of fairness 'is intended to apply to such private associations' (ibid.).

This leads to the further question of what is to count as a contribution to the organisation. This depends on the *ends* or objectives which the organisation chooses to pursue, as surely by definition a contribution (as opposed to a detriment) cannot contradict the ends of the organisation. A proponent of the shareholder view might subscribe to the principle of fairness, but identify 'merit' in terms of a contribution to the maximisation of shareholder value. This is indeed the position of Sternberg (2000: 80–2). As she puts it, 'what is fair or just according to distributive justice is always relative to the defining purpose of a particular organisation' (2000: 81) and 'The definitive purpose of a business is to maximise long-term owner value by selling goods and services; promotions and pay rises should therefore go to those who contribute most to owner value' (2000: 80). Her formulation of distributive justice, however, looks almost

---

[20] On this point he writes, 'Contracts are notoriously incomplete. Employment contracts cannot possibly state in advance every duty of an employee, even at the lowest levels of the organization. Some stakeholder relationships are not the subject of formal contracts. Many small transactions with customers do not require contracts. Nor are the organization's obligations to local communities always the subject of a formal contracting process' (2003: 93).

identical to that of Phillips (2003): 'organizational rewards should be proportional to contributions made to organisational ends' (2000: 80). So the principle of fairness can only help to justify a stakeholder theory of the corporate objective if a separate argument is provided for what this objective should be. In other words, the principle of fairness is by itself unable to provide a normative basis for stakeholder theory.[21] However, the possibility of this sort of principle as a normative basis remains important in a consideration of the different philosophies that stakeholder theory might draw upon, and for this reason the principle of fairness is returned to in the next chapter.

Conclusion

This chapter has traced the development of the stakeholder idea from its earliest use in the English language, through its passage into organisation theory and its development into a body of normative theory. It has been necessary to consider the different uses of the stakeholder concept in an instrumental and normative context, and in the political sense of a 'stakeholder economy'. From this point on, the version of the theory engaged with is that which articulates a *normative* theory of the corporate objective and has the effect of lending legitimacy to

---

[21] Phillips (2003: 75) does have an argument for what the corporate objective should be. Drawing on the work of Thomas A. Smith (1999), Phillips argues that hypothetically the rational investor 'would own not only stocks, but also bonds and other forms of debt. They would not want to see the equity investment (i.e., common stock) privileged to the detriment of these other forms of debt unless the increase in the value of the equity were greater than the decrease in the value of the other forms of debt. In other words... rational investors would want managers to act so as to maximize the value of all claims on the corporation'. The 'objective' of the corporation, for Phillips (2003), is therefore simultaneously to maximise the claims that all investors have against it. The theory is not dealt with here in any detail because it appears implausible. Can a corporation negotiate a fixed claim with any particular stakeholder (a bank, worker, supplier, etc) without a prior objective to serve as a benchmark for arriving at an acceptable claim? In other words, an objective (e.g. to maximise profits) in terms of which stakeholder claims are evaluated? An objective to maximise all stakeholder claims simultaneously could only have a rational solution if a corporation possessed infinite wealth; otherwise the claims it agreed to would have to be balanced somehow, and a prior objective (not reducible to maximising everyone's wealth) would be needed as a guide for arriving at this balance.

CSR as a moral goal. As this book asks whether a justification of stakeholder theory is conceptually consistent with the ethical framework of a market economy, it is these theories that are examined through the rest of the book. To enquire into the validity of these arguments, the philosophical assumptions upon which they rest are now brought to light.

3 | *The philosophy of stakeholder theory*

Chapter 2 expounded a range of normative arguments employed in defence of a stakeholder theory of the firm. What this chapter engages with are the philosophical ideas that underpin the attempts to find a normative justification for stakeholder theory. By 'underpin' I do not refer to the full range of ideologies that might in any way have influenced writing on stakeholder theory. Instead, the discussion is limited to the ideas and authors that are explicitly appealed to as sources of authority in the leading texts of stakeholder theory.

What is assumed in applying the idea of a 'social contract' is that all the stakeholders of a corporation can be considered as part of a joint association, which is to be regulated by terms that are consistent with the consent of all individuals who are part of it. Any argument drawing on Rawls in particular or the social contract tradition in general (at least in its individualist form after Hobbes) must have this sort of outline if it is to defend distributive principles at the level of the corporation. The focus here is on the aspects of social contract theory that are pertinent to a stakeholder conception of the firm, and how Rawls employs the social contract method to defend his two principles of justice, which are in turn taken up by stakeholder theorists.

Of the four branches of argument referred to, the second concludes that instead of being run in the interests of shareholders, business corporations should have as their objective the 'public interest'. However, the philosophical basis of these arguments is not examined separately from that of those that employ the explicit social contract approach. Rawls and Rousseau are cited by Boatright (1994) and McNulty (1975), and the only difference between these stakeholder theorists and those of the first group appears to be that in the first case a *limited* set of stakeholders constitute the association whose joint interests form the corporate objective, and in the second the *whole* of 'society' is included.[1] The units differ but the frameworks of the arguments are similar enough for their philosophical foundations to be treated as the same.

The third and fourth branches cannot so easily be treated under the same categories. Donaldson and Preston (1995) do not invoke a social contract method for their defence of stakeholder theory.[2] Instead, they cite recent work on the theory of property (e.g. Munzer, 1990 and Becker, 1992) to support their argument that claim-rights to property are not self-evident and must be underpinned by principles of distributive justice. The difficulty with this view, to be explored later, is that it is not immediately clear whether distributive justice is merely a constraint on the use of corporate property for the interests of shareholders, or would actually replace the shareholder objective with a different corporate goal. Perhaps this turns on whether the corporation is itself the site of distributive justice, in which managers have the moral discretion for acting on these principles, or whether the pursuit of the corporate objective merely has *legal* constraints that derive their legitimacy from these principles, but with a scope that goes beyond the corporation itself.

The same set of questions can be asked of the fourth branch of argument, that of the principle of fairness. As argued above, Phillips's argument (2003) that corporations incur a reciprocal obligation towards stakeholders in proportion to benefits received could be consistent with the shareholder objective if the principle of fairness is merely a moral or legal *constraint* on the pursuit of this goal. However, the corporation could be seen as responsible not just for adhering to fair principles in the transactions it conducts with stakeholders in the name of shareholders, but for *determining* what counts as fair between stakeholders, and for moving resources from one stakeholder to another as fairness demands. This would be analogous to how a legislative

---

[1] In a more recent article, Reynolds and Yuthas (2008: 50) make the straightforward assumption that all applications of social contract theory are of this type: 'Social contract theory emphasizes that corporations come into being to provide social goods and services and are incorporated by government, and thus by the people. This legal incorporation establishes all of society as stakeholders'.

[2] This is notwithstanding Donaldson's work with Thomas Dunfee in developing their 'Integrative Social Contracts Theory' as a framework for understanding corporate obligations (Donaldson and Dunfee 1994, 1995, 1999).

authority might regulate the distribution of goods between the citizens of a state.

This is also a way of interpreting the application of distributive justice to the corporation. The corporation might be regulated by a law which compels it to act in ways that effect a just pattern of distribution (e.g., to pay a certain rate of taxation or pay a minimum wage), or within the law managers might act from a moral impulse to treat stakeholders equitably (e.g., through employee pay rises, or contributions to the local community, or voluntary action on the environment), but each of these could simply be a set of constraints within which managers attempt to maximise shareholder wealth. However, if managers had something analogous to a sovereign power to settle issues of distributive justice between stakeholders[3] and to override the moral judgement of stakeholders themselves, then this would entail an objective very different to that of shareholder wealth. However, for reasons that will emerge, if management is to wield this power legitimately, the firm must be conceived of as an association of stakeholders formed around a common objective. It turns out that the same issues that arise in applying the social contract method to the corporation could also arise with the principles of fairness[4] and distributive justice. Therefore, it is appropriate to turn now to the social contract tradition of political theory.

Social contract theory

Most of the stakeholder arguments considered in Chapter 2 draw not on 'social contract' theory generally but on the work of John Rawls in particular. Rawls is, however, unambiguous about his own relation to the social contract tradition: 'What I have attempted to do is to generalise and carry to a higher order of abstraction the traditional

---

[3] As in Hobbes's (1651/1996: 100) understanding of the concept: 'And distributive justice, the justice of an arbitrator; that is to say, the act of defining what is just. Wherein (being trusted by them that make him arbitrator), if he perform his trust, he is said to distribute to every man his own: and this is indeed just distribution'.

[4] In fact, as shown later, the 'principle of fairness' as Phillips (2003) employs it (which he borrows from Rawls) does not lend itself to the problem of 'social' or 'distributive' justice at the level of the state, but instead applies to private voluntary associations.

theory of the social contract as represented by Locke, Rousseau, and Kant' (1999: xviii). It is possible to see the attention given to Rawls as legitimised by the general idea that corporations can be spoken of in terms of a 'social contract'. Donaldson and Dunfee's (1994, 1995, 1999) work on the application of different forms of social contract to business ethics, which they synthesise in their 'Integrative Social Contracts Theory', is at the heart of much scholarly interest in the idea.

Höpfl and Thompson (1979) highlight the uncertainty amongst scholars of the social contract as to what the sources for this body of thought are,[5] and which writers and writings can properly be said to be part of it. They write, 'even Hobbes, Locke and Rousseau have had their credentials for inclusion challenged, directly or by implication' (1979: 921). However, as stated above, the 'traditional theory' that Rawls sees himself working with is that of Locke, Rousseau and Kant, and he regards these authors as 'definitive of the social contract tradition' (1999: 10).[6] This discussion of social contract theory will focus on these modern and early modern writers, as they are the contractarian inspiration behind Rawls's theory of justice. Therefore,

[5] They write, 'Opinions have differed widely about the sources and appeal of contractarian argument in the early modern period ... the following possible sources have been mentioned: Old Testament history; medieval references to contracts and feudal understandings of social and political relations; the teachings of the Church Fathers; the ideas of the Conciliar movement; Lutheran and Calvinist ideas and practices; texts of the civil law; the supposed constitutional arrangements of ancient city states and the Roman Republic; the past and more recent constitutions of the German Empire, Aragon, Switzerland, Poland, and Holland; the gradual breakdown of the extended family; the rise of capitalism; the rise of individualism and rationalism; and the impact of the scientific revolution of the seventeenth century. In the debate about the relative significance of these presumed origins, rarely has an author singled out one source for the rise of modern European contractualism' (1979: 920).

[6] He alludes to the inclusion of Hobbes, but adds: 'For all its greatness, Hobbes's *Leviathan* raises special problems' (ibid.). I will, however, treat Hobbes as part of this tradition, because the writings of the contractual authors that follow him can scarcely be understood outside the context of his work. According to Höpfl and Thompson (1979: 940), the conceptual device of a 'State of Nature' was the invention of Hobbes, and 'The history of contractualism subsequent to Hobbes is, indeed, in part a record of the adaptations and modifications of the language Hobbes consolidated', and this is the language 'in which the famous contractualist treatises of Pufendorf, Spinoza, Locke, Thomasius, Christian Wolff, Vattel, Rousseau, and Fichte were written' (1979: 941).

in the context of stakeholder theory and the influence of Rawls's work upon it, it is here that one might look for the philosophical principles of this body of political theory.

A point of consensus in this tradition is that if individuals are faced with a 'State of Nature' in which no coercive political power exists, they would be rational to give up the freedom to protect their own rights and to judge their own cases when their rights are threatened by others. They contract out this freedom to a common over-arching power which has equal legitimacy for all who enter the contract.[7] The role of this common power is to achieve the mutual purpose for which the contract is formed in the first place, to remedy the key defect of the 'State of Nature', which is held to be the threat to a person's own preservation. An important point here is the basis of the social contract in voluntary *consent*, rather than in the inevitable consequences of a teleological or determinist theory of human behaviour or history.[8]

Perhaps the first theorist to make a clear break with the teleological tradition of the Middle Ages in favour of a contract for the state founded on conscious human will was the German Calvinist Johannes Althusius. In assessing Otto von Gierke's belief that Althusius was the first 'genuine' theorist of the social contract, Höpfl and Thompson (1979: 924) write: 'Althusius's system explained the state purely in terms of individual human willing and thus broke completely with the Christian and Aristotelian traditions'. However, they point out that 'The bearers of rights in his conception are still unmistakeably associations, groups, and corporations of various sorts, not individuals' and that a covenant between individuals was not one that he

---

[7] The exception is often assumed to apply where no recourse to political power is possible, as in the case of immediate self-defence. On this point, Hobbes (1651/1996: 87) writes that a general rule of reason is that '*every man, ought to endeavour peace, as far as he has hope of obtaining it; and when he cannot obtain it, that he may seek, and use, all helps, and advantages of war*' (emphasis in original). Hobbes calls the second branch of this rule 'the sum of the Right of Nature; which is, *by all means we can, to defend ourselves*' (ibid., emphasis in original). Locke (1689/1988: 280) also speaks of the 'Right of War' under which one is permitted to kill an aggressor if he or she leaves no time to appeal to a common judge.

[8] As will be seen in Chapter 4, the compatibility of stakeholder theory with a market economy depends on the extent to which stakeholders *consent* to the form of association necessary for a legitimate stakeholder objective.

contemplated (1979: 936). The tradition in which Rawls's work is situated is, however, individualist, in the sense that his theory of justice is an attempt to find principles for the regulation of the basic structure of society from the perspective of an individual situated behind the veil of ignorance.[9]

It is possible to identify Hobbes as the first writer to work out a theory of the social contract in terms of individual human will. Höpfl and Thompson (1979: 936) write that in contrast with Althusius, 'this is the covenant that Hobbes made into a durable form of political argument'. The role of voluntary consent, despite differences in how this is defined, is clear in the contractual theory of Hobbes and all the writers of the tradition to which Rawls belongs. Hobbes writes that the definition of *injustice* is the non-performance of covenants (1651/1996: 95) and that an injustice is 'voluntarily to undo that, which from the beginning he had voluntarily done' (1651/1996: 88). He makes clear the *voluntary* nature of the covenant of 'every man with every man' (1651/1996: 114) which is essential in the formation of a commonwealth, whether by institution (1651/1996: 115) or by acquisition, in which a man consents to be the subject of a conqueror (1651/1996: 468). It is also clear in the preface to Locke's *Two Treatises of Government*, in which he writes that his papers should be sufficient to establish the throne of King William in the *consent* of the people, which he argues is the only basis of all lawful governments (1689/1988: 137). The same emphasis is present in Rousseau's (1762/1968: 59) 'Original Covenant', in which there must be the assumption of an original *unanimous agreement* to bind the minority of the body politic to the vote of the majority; and in Kant's argument that as no wrong is done to someone who *consents*, 'only the concurring and united will of all, insofar as each decides the same thing for all and all for each, and so only the general united will of the people, can be legislative' (1797/1996: 91). Finally, the voluntary consent of the autonomous individual is central to Rawls's own theory: 'a society satisfying the principles of justice as fairness comes as close as a society can to being a voluntary scheme, for it meets the principles which free and equal persons would assent to under circumstances that are fair. In this sense its

---

[9] To be more accurate, the parties in the original position are not literally single individuals, nor are they associations either, but 'continuing persons', meaning family heads or genetic lines (1999: 126).

members are autonomous and the obligations they recognise self-imposed' (1999: 12).

On the assumption of the consent of every individual subject to it, it is held that the sovereign power created has the right to use the property and resources of its subjects for the common purpose underpinning the contract itself. It follows that the discretion to decide how to use the property of the members of the association (or citizens of the state) for the achievement of this common purpose must, within the constraints of consent and the rule of law, be held exclusively by the common power. If the judgement of any individual citizen could override the common power (otherwise called the *sovereign*) then the entire purpose of the social contract would collapse. This is why Hobbes (1651/1996: 119) asserts that as a basic right of sovereignty, the sovereign has the whole power of 'prescribing the rules, whereby every man may know, what goods he may enjoy, and what actions he may do'. It is also the basis for Kant's claim that the sovereign is to be regarded as the supreme proprietor of the land (1797/1996: 99).

However, in asserting the rights of the sovereign created for the common purpose for which all individuals voluntarily unite, one might well ask what this common purpose is supposed to be. Without the assumption of a unifying purpose which would command the assent of all members of the social contract, the logical implications derived from it would come to nought. In considering whether this whole style of argument can be applied to a business corporation, it is essential to look first at *why* the writers of this tradition feel that individuals would wish to establish a sovereign power in the first place.

For Hobbes (1651/1996: 67) it is the fear of oppression from others that places our lives and security at so great a risk that there is no remedy but to form a society, and submit to political power for our mutual protection. He writes: 'Fear of oppression, disposeth a man to anticipate, or to seek aid by society: for there is no other way by which a man can secure himself his life and liberty'. Why is it that a man should fear the oppression of his fellow men, and seek to alleviate this? Hobbes (1651/1996: 82) answers that men are by nature *equal*; and by this he means relatively equal in strength[10] and,

---

[10] Hobbes (1651/1996: 82) writes, 'as to the strength of the body, the weakest has strength enough to kill the strongest, either by secret machination, or by confederacy with others, that are in the same danger with himself'.

crucially, in opinion of their own wisdom. The latter is because prudence, which gives man a vain conceit of his own wisdom, is for Hobbes nothing more than experience, 'which equal time, equally bestows on all men, in those things they equally apply themselves unto' (ibid.).

Hobbes reasons that from this relative equality of strength and opinion of our own wisdom, arises equality of *hope* in attaining our ends (1651/1996: 83). He is driven to the conclusion that 'if any two men desire the same thing, which nevertheless they cannot both enjoy, they become enemies; and in the way to their end . . . endeavour to destroy, or subdue one another' (ibid.). The implication is that man must try to gather enough power around him to be secure of his own conservation, and is driven to use violence to invade others both for personal gain, and for the safety of what he has gained already (1651/1996: 83–4). Hobbes argues famously that this is tantamount to 'that condition which is called war; and such a war, as if of every man, against every man' (1651/1996: 84). For this reason men must submit to a common power to hold them all in awe, to prevent the causes of quarrel and threats to security that arise among them, because if they have no security but their own strength, then their lives are 'solitary, poor, nasty, brutish and short' (ibid.).

From these observations Hobbes sets out his second law of nature,[11] which is 'that a man be willing, when others are so too, as far-forth, as for peace, and defence of himself he shall think it necessary, to lay down this right to all things;[12] and be contented with so much liberty against other men, as he would allow other men against himself' (1651/1996: 87). For these reasons it is rational for men to give up their natural right to govern themselves and to submit to a common power which enforces order and is the final judge of conflicts between the people. Hobbes is quick to assert that the only motive for giving up one's rights is self-preservation and for no other end are any rights transferred. In fact Hobbes declares that if a man appears to transfer a right for

---

[11] A 'law of nature' is for Hobbes a general rule 'found out by reason, by which a man is forbidden to do, that, which is destructive of his life, or taketh away the means of preserving the same' (1651/1996: 86).

[12] Hobbes refers here to his earlier observation that in the natural condition of man, 'every man has a right to every thing; even to one another's body. And therefore, as long as this natural right of every man to every thing endureth, there can be no security to any man' (1651/1996: 87).

any other purpose, then he cannot be understood as if he meant it (1651/1996: 88–9).

A similar though less analytical line of argument can be found in John Locke's *Second Treatise of Government*. Locke (1689/1988: 350) asks why man would be inclined to give up his natural freedom in the 'State of Nature' and submit to the power of political society. He answers, 'though in the state of Nature he hath such a right [to his own person and possessions], yet the Enjoyment of it is very uncertain, and constantly exposed to the Invasion of others'. Locke argues that man has a reason to leave the 'State of Nature', for the sole purpose of protecting his life, liberty and estates, which he calls by the general name 'Property' (1689/1988: 350). He argues that the only situation in which one divests one's self of one's natural liberty and puts on the bonds of civil society 'is by agreeing with other Men to joyn and unite into a Community, for their comfortable, safe, and peaceable living one amongst another, in a secure Enjoyment of their Properties, and a greater Security against any that are not of it' (1689/1988: 331).

A broadly similar position is found in the other writers of the social contract tradition. Rousseau in *The Social Contract* writes that 'Man's first law is to watch over his own preservation; his first care he owes to himself' (1762/1968: 50). In explaining 'The Social Pact' he argues that only 'by uniting their separate powers in a combination strong enough to overcome any resistance' can men ensure their own preservation (1762/1968: 59–60). Later he asserts, perhaps showing the influence of Hobbes,[13] that one is at far greater peril in the 'State of Nature', 'where every man is inevitably at war' (1762/1968: 78). Likewise, Immanuel Kant, in discussing the state of affairs logically prior to a public constitution, writes: 'before a public lawful condition is established individual human beings, peoples, and states can never be secure against violence from one another, since each has its own right to do *what seems right and good to it*' (1797/1996: 89–90, emphasis in original).[14]

---

[13] For a brief account of the possible influence of Hobbes's thought on Rousseau, see Cranston (1968: 26–7).

[14] In his earlier essay *On the Common Saying: 'This may be true in theory, but it does not apply in practice'*, Kant (1793/1991: 90) expresses a similar view: 'universal violence and the distress it produces must eventually make a people decide to submit to the coercion which reason itself prescribes (i.e. coercion of public law), and to enter into a *civil* constitution' (emphasis in original).

The problem of the private judgement of rights to which Kant alludes in this passage will be discussed shortly. What is apparent in the arguments of these writers is that human nature is such that for individuals wishing to preserve their rights it is rational to limit their freedom by submission to the authority of a political power. There are great differences between these writers in their epistemological assumptions as to how political power is justified, and the extent to which subjects may retain judgement over their own rights in a dispute with the state. Locke (1689/1988: 406–27) and Kant (1797/1996: 96–8), for example, come to exactly opposite conclusions on the subject's right of rebellion. However, the common purpose of mutual protection for the sake of which it is rational for individuals to form a common power is a consistent point of agreement amongst these writers.

A further implication of this political right to regulate and secure the ownership of property is the right of the common power to resolve *disputes* between subjects with regard to their property. For Hobbes this imperative stems from the limitations of a man's reason with respect to any item of disputed knowledge. He writes:

No man's reason, nor the reason of any one number of men, makes the certainty ... therefore, as when there is a controversy in account, the parties must by their own accord, set up for right reason, the reason of some arbitrator, or judge, to whose sentence they will both stand, or their controversy must either come to blows, or be undecided ... so it is in all debates of what kind soever. (1651/1996: 28)

As in scientific questions, Hobbes extends this insight to cover questions of good and evil as well. Having asserted that there is nothing simply and absolutely good and evil, and that these names are used only in relation to the person that uses these words, he writes that there is no common rule for good and evil to be taken from the nature of objects themselves, 'but from the person of the man (where there is no common-wealth;) or, (in a common-wealth,) from the person that representeth it; or from an arbitrator or judge, whom men disagreeing shall by consent set up, and make his sentence the rule thereof' (1651/1996: 35). It follows for Hobbes that two laws of nature are to be observed:[15] that no man is his own judge and that 'no man be judge, that has in him a natural cause of partiality' (1651/1996: 104).

---

[15] Laws of nature for Hobbes are to be observed *in foro interno* (in conscience) always, but outside a state of security man will become the prey of others if he

For Locke (1689/1988: 281) the want of a common judge is a key distinction between the 'State of Nature' and political society (see also 1689/1988: 324, 351). He writes that one great reason for men quitting the 'State of Nature' and putting themselves into society is that 'where there is an Authority, a Power on Earth, from which relief can be had by *appeal*, there the continuance of the State of War is excluded, and the Controversie is decided by that Power' (1689/1988: 282, emphasis in original). The key point is that for Locke, as stated earlier, the chief end of men uniting into a commonwealth and putting themselves under a government is the preservation of their property (1689/1988: 350–1), and for many reasons the 'State of Nature' is wanting in this respect. Chief among these is that

In the State of Nature there wants a *known and indifferent Judge*, with Authority to determine all differences according to the Established Law. For every one in that state being both Judge and Executioner of the Law of Nature,[16] Men being partial to themselves, Passion and Revenge is very apt to carry them too far, and with too much heat, in their own Cases. (1689/1988: 351, emphases in original)

A similar insistence that the private judgement of rights belongs to a condition outside civil society, and that once a political power is formed its role is to adjudicate disputes between the opposing claims of individuals, is also assumed by Rousseau, Kant and Rawls's Harvard contemporary Robert Nozick. Rousseau (1762/1968: 60–1) argues that an individual member (or 'associate') of society cannot *claim* any rights that he or she may have possessed outside society, because individuals in society can no longer judge their own cases; if they could, then the 'State of Nature' would be kept in being. Kant's view is that because there is no judge in the 'State of Nature' with the rightful power to pass a verdict when rights are in dispute, there can be no justice in this condition, and people can thus compel each other *by force* to leave the 'State of Nature' and enter the 'civil condition' (1797/1996: 90).

---

alone follows these rules. Therefore having obtained a condition of peace, man must always follow the laws of nature not only in conscience but also in his external actions, *in foro externo* (1651/1996: 104).

[16] Locke (1689/1988: 271) writes at the outset of his argument that 'the *Execution* of the Law of Nature is in that State, put into every Mans hands, whereby every one has a right to punish transgressors of that Law to such a Degree, as may hinder its Violation' (emphasis in original).

For Kant one major benefit of the civil condition and the exercise of political power is that there is necessarily a third party under which an impartial adjudication of rights can be made.

Furthermore, Robert Nozick (1974), in his attempt to show how a state with a monopoly on the enforcement of rights can arise through an 'invisible hand' process in which individuals are concerned only with the protection of their natural (Lockean) rights, reasons as follows: 'Presumably what drives people to use the state's system of justice is the issue of ultimate enforcement. Only the state can enforce a judgement against the will of one of the parties. For the state does not *allow* anyone else to enforce another system's judgement' (1974: 14, emphasis in original).

The consistency in all these arguments is that if the legitimate exercise of political power depends on the state's ability to protect the rights of its citizens, then it is also legitimate for it to act as the final judge in adjudicating and settling disputes over rights. As Hobbes (1651/1996: 379) puts it: 'Jurisdiction is the power of hearing and determining causes between man and man; and can belong to none, but him who hath the power to prescribe the rules of right and wrong; that is, to make laws'. This gives sense to the idea that political power must be *singular* in any one state, with the implication of a monopoly on the right to adjudicate conflicts between its citizens.[17] If this were not so, and there were two separate judiciaries in a state with *equal* authority, this would not be the kind of authority that could be exercised as a *final* judgement on disputes – as there would always be a competing source of authority.

It could be argued that in the presence today of international law and international courts, such as the European Court of Human Rights, the 'social contract' theory of state sovereignty has diminished in relevance. If a nation-state has become subject to a higher legal authority, then can it any longer be described as 'sovereign'? The answer to this question seems to depend on whether states still possess legitimate authority to recognise and implement law in their own territory. Michael Oakeshott (2006: 368), discussing the emergence of modern

---

[17] This is not to enter the debate about whether the legislative, judicial and executive powers of the state should lie in separate hands, a point on which there is disagreement among these authors.

European political thought, writes that a 'sovereign' state is an 'associ-ation whose government is not legally obliged to any other, or higher, authority unless it *expressly accepts* such an obligation' (emphasis added).[18] This understanding suggests that the authority of interna-tional law stems from the sovereignty of independent states. This is broadly consistent, for example, with the authority of the European Convention on Human Rights. The rights protected by the Conven-tion are those that states 'have undertaken to secure and guarantee to everyone within their jurisdiction', and protocols adding rights to the Convention 'are binding only on those States [sic] that have signed and ratified them' (Public Relations Unit 2012: 5). Furthermore, it is the obligation of *states* to execute the judgements of the Court and the obligation of the Committee of Ministers to 'confer with the country concerned . . . to decide how the judgment should be executed and how to prevent similar violations of the Convention in the future' (Public Relations Unit 2012: 10).

International human rights law provides further examples of the power of a sovereign state to define its own obligation to a 'higher' legal authority. Smith (2009: 28) writes that 'even when a state accepts a particular human rights treaty, it can still avoid full legal responsibil-ity by a variety of legal means.' These include the entering of a 'reser-vation' by a state after ratification of a treaty. She gives the following example:

Saudi Arabia's statement on ratification of the *Convention on Elimination of All Forms of Discrimination against Women* that, in the event of a conflict between the Convention and Islamic law, the Kingdom would not be obliged to follow the Convention. Although objected to by a number of European states, the Saudi reservation remains in force. (Smith 2009: 31)

Smith (2009: 33) goes on to add: 'Although the concept of reserva-tions appears inconsistent with that of human rights treaties, little action is taken against states entering and maintaining reservations . . . This is a perennial problem with a consensus-based system such as international law'. If sovereign states still create, implement and enforce international law and in so doing determine its boundaries and

---

[18] The contrast is with a medieval political community: 'a medieval king whose acts as a ruler were subject to the legal veto of a pope or an emperor, was not a sovereign ruler' (ibid.).

effectiveness, then it would seem premature to regard the 'social contract' theory of sovereignty as an anachronism.[19]

Putting together the two axioms of the social contract approach so far described, that of the voluntary consent of all subjects in forming an association whose purpose is equally valid for all, and the need for an independent judicial authority, a further implication is the *rule of law*. This is the simple idea that legislation must apply to all subjects qua subject, hence equally for all who are subject to the law, and not in the light of one's particular characteristics or personal circumstances. Closely allied to this is the view that all law must be made public, so that the subjects of a state can plan their lives in the knowledge of what they may be constrained to do by law and what they may not. Whether the publicity of law is conceptually entailed by the rule of law is not a question that can be addressed adequately here, but it is a fact that the two have often been argued for together in this tradition of political theory.

These two principles are a constant feature of Locke's *Second Treatise of Government*. The freedom of men under government is, he argues, 'to have a standing Rule to live by, common to every one of that Society, and made by the Legislative Power erected in it', and not to be subject to the arbitrary will of another man (1689/1988: 284). He adds that *liberty* is to be free to dispose of our persons and property within the allowance of the laws (1689/1988: 306), and the *capacity of knowing* a law is what makes a man free to act according to his own will, within the permission of that law (1689/1988: 307). In writing of the formation of political society, he argues: 'All private judgement of every particular Member being excluded, the Community comes to be Umpire, by settled standing Rules, indifferent, and the same to all Parties' (1689/1988: 324). Exclaiming that to live under arbitrary power is worse than being in the 'State of Nature', he argues 'the Ruling Power ought to govern by declared and received Laws, and not

---

[19] The existence of international law indeed poses difficult questions for the concept of sovereignty which the early theorists of the social contract did not have to confront. Much more can of course be said on this issue, for example, regarding extraordinary cases where in the event of egregious human rights violations, such as genocide, states can be argued to have surrendered their sovereignty. See also the robust argument by Skinner (2009) on the continuing need for a theory of the sovereign state. I would like to thank Jeremy Moon and Edzia Carvalho for helping to clarify my understanding of these issues.

by extemporary Dictates and undetermined Resolutions' (1689/1988: 360).

A parallel argument can be found in Rousseau's (1762/1968: 77) insistence that the sovereign, if its acts are to be general and not private, can never impose a greater burden on one than on another. For Hobbes (1651/1996: 103), the eleventh law of nature is *equity*, about which he writes: 'if *a man be trusted to judge between man and man*, it is a precept of the law of nature, *that he deal equally between them*' (emphases in original). He unequivocally endorses the rule of law as applying equally to all, when he writes that the safety of the people is *not* to be achieved by care applied to individuals, 'but by a general providence... in the making and executing of good laws, to which individual persons may apply their own cases' (1651/1996: 222). It is for this reason, for example, that Hobbes proposes an equal payment of tax from all members of a commonwealth, regardless of individual wealth (1651/1996: 229).

Therefore, it seems that at least three principles underpin the regulation of individuals and their property in the social contract tradition. First, there is a common purpose for which individuals jointly and freely consent to give up some of their rights to a common power. Second, as a logical implication of there being a single common power with the right to compel its subjects in the name of the common purpose, a single judicial authority has the right to decide controversies between them. And third, if all members are assumed to consent voluntarily to this common power, then any laws passed for the regulation of this association must apply equally to all.

Setting out these principles and their implications in detail illustrates the coherence of the contract approach when applied to the problem of political legitimacy and the state, and thus what criteria a stakeholder conception of the firm would have to meet if it is to use these philosophies as a foundation. Now I turn to the philosopher whose work has been more directly influential in the field of stakeholder theory than any other.

John Rawls and social contract theory

Before I give a brief outline of the argument Rawls makes in favour of his two principles of justice, it should be noted that he does not differ in any major respect from the basic principles of traditional social contract theory covered in the preceding. Also, on the common purpose for the sake of which individuals join together in society, Rawls does not depart from the traditional explanation of mutual protection. In discussing the 'Circumstances of Justice', which 'may be described as the normal conditions under which human cooperation is both possible and necessary' (1999: 109), Rawls echoes Hobbes in asserting that no single individual is able to dominate the rest: 'They are vulnerable to attack, and all are subject to having their plans blocked by the united force of others' (ibid.). Elsewhere he writes that 'even in a well ordered society the coercive powers of government are to some degree necessary for the stability of social cooperation' (1999: 211), and in another echo of Hobbes (1651/1996: 91) and Rousseau (1762/1968: 63), he writes that this is because men lack full confidence in one another that each will do their part in the absence of a coercive power.

On the need for a single judicial authority, Rawls says that it is part of men's natural situation that 'their judgement is likely to be distorted by anxiety, bias, and a preoccupation with their own affairs' (1999: 110), and furthermore that it is part of 'natural justice' that judges be impartial and no one may judge in his or her own case (1999: 210). Rawls also openly advocates what I have referred to as the *rule of law*. When describing the impartial and consistent administration of laws and institutions as *formal justice*, he writes: 'If we think of justice as expressing a kind of equality, then formal justice requires that in their administration laws and institutions should apply equally (that is, in the same way) to those belonging to the classes defined by them' (1999: 51). He is equally clear that the principles of justice for the regulation and distribution of property are incorrectly applied if they become the direct concern of individuals: 'neither principle applies to distributions of particular goods to particular individuals who may be identified by their proper names. The situation where someone is considering how to allocate certain commodities to needy persons who are known to him is not within the scope of the principles. They are meant to regulate basic institutional arrangements' (1999: 56). This mirrors the claims of other social contract theorists that the regulation of property can be the concern only of the sovereign power to which all have consented, and that the basic liberty of the individual is at risk without this safeguard against arbitrary invasions of property.

I now move to a direct discussion of the two principles of justice, and the reasoning underlying them. Rawls explains at the outset of *A Theory of Justice* that his aim is to argue for the principles of justice that should govern the 'basic structure of society' (1999: 3). In other words, he is primarily interested in *social* justice rather what should count as just between individuals. By society's 'basic structure' he refers to the way in which the 'major social institutions' distribute rights and duties and determine the division of the advantages of social cooperation between individuals (1999: 6). These institutions, such as the political constitution and the principal economic and social arrangements (such as markets and systems of property), are those that define the rights and duties of individuals and influence their life prospects (ibid.). This then is the subject of Rawls's theory, and he makes it clear that any conception of justice would recognise that: 'institutions are just when no arbitrary distinctions are made between persons in the assigning of basic rights and duties and when the rules determine a proper balance between competing claims to the advantages of social life' (1999: 5).

If this is the problem that Rawls sets himself, then how does he think it should be solved? His contention is that the principles of justice would be those that free and rational persons concerned to further their own interests would accept in an initial position of equality, defining the 'fundamental terms' of their association (1999: 10). He explains that this original position of equality is 'a purely hypothetical situation characterised so as to lead to a certain conception of justice'[20] (1999: 11). By 'equality' he means that no one is advantaged or disadvantaged in the choice of principles by natural choice or contingency of social circumstance, so that no one can choose principles to favour their own particular position (ibid.). The intention is to leave aside those aspects of the social world that seem 'arbitrary' from a moral point of view, and to prevent 'the use of the accidents of endowment and the contingencies of social circumstance as counters in a quest for political and economic advantage' (1999: 14). The normative starting point for Rawls is therefore that of *moral equality* between human beings.

[20] Hypothetical in the sense that there is not any assembly of people who actually bargain from behind a veil of ignorance; instead it is a position that can be entered at any time by any individual, simply by following the procedure of arguing for principles of justice in accordance with the restrictions of the original position (1999: 17).

The implication of this conjectural original position is that individuals entering society are situated behind a 'veil of ignorance' in which they know general facts about society (which are not morally 'arbitrary') such as generally accepted theories of economics and human psychology (1999: 119), but as moral equals they do not know anything to distinguish them from other human beings, such as their place in society (i.e., class position or social status), their natural assets or abilities (e.g., intelligence or strength), their conception of the good, their risk preferences, the level of civilisation or culture of their society, or the generation to which they belong (1999: 118). He confirms that the purpose of these conditions 'is to represent equality between human beings as moral persons, as creatures having a conception of the good and capable of a sense of justice', and that his theory does not rank in value the particular ends which individuals pursue (1999: 17).

The principles he believes would be chosen in this initial situation by a group of persons who 'must decide once and for all what is to count among them as just or unjust' (1999: 11) are as follows. There are two principles, the first of which is that 'each person is to have an equal right to the most extensive scheme of equal basic liberties compatible with a similar scheme of liberties for others' (1999: 53). This is to capture the idea of the inviolability of each individual, such that no individuals would consent to give up their most basic rights and liberties in exchange for an overall increase in social welfare, which lies at the root of Rawls's many criticisms of utilitarianism. As chosen from behind the veil of ignorance, these liberties must be held *equally*, and include the right to vote and hold public office (political liberty), freedom of speech and assembly, liberty of conscience and freedom of thought, freedom of the person from psychological oppression and physical assault, 'the right to hold personal property and freedom from arbitrary arrest and seizure as defined by the rule of law' (ibid.).

The second principle is designed to alleviate the effects of natural and social contingencies on the position of individuals in the distribution of income and wealth, which individuals do not 'deserve' and which would be arbitrary from a moral point of view. Rawls argues that with the constraint of equal basic liberties, which being inviolable the second principle cannot override, 'Social and economic inequalities are to be arranged so that they are both (a) to the greatest expected benefit of the least advantaged and (b) attached to offices and positions open to all under conditions of fair equality of opportunity'[21] (1999: 72). He explains this principle as follows: 'While the distribution of wealth and income need not be equal, it must be to everyone's advantage, and at the same time positions of authority and responsibility must be accessible to all' (1999: 53). Subject to the constraints of equal liberties and positions of authority being open to all, social and economic inequalities are to be arranged so that everyone benefits. This expresses the Kantian idea that

To regard persons as ends in themselves in the basic design of society is to agree to forgo those gains which do not contribute to everyone's expectations. By contrast to regard persons as means is to be prepared to impose on those already less favoured still lower prospects of life for the sake of the higher expectations of others. (1999: 157)

One might ask why treating persons as ends in themselves would entail an *equal* distribution of rights, liberties, opportunities and income and wealth, unless (in the latter case) they led to an improvement in everyone's position. The reasoning Rawls offers is that in an original position of moral equality and without the assumption of altruism,[22] it would not be rational for someone to agree to a *less* than average share of primary social goods, and as he cannot claim a *greater* than average share, the first step is to assume an *equal* distribution. This means that everyone has equal basic liberties, equality of fair opportunity and an equal share of income and wealth (1999: 130). However, as people are not assumed to be motivated by envy (as regards selecting principles of justice), inequalities of income are permitted if they improve everyone's

---

[21] The principle of 'fair equality of opportunity' is to remedy the effects of social contingencies on people's life prospects, which means 'positions are to be not only open in a formal sense, but that all should have a fair chance to attain them' (1999: 63). This still leaves the problem of 'natural contingency' which Rawls's 'difference principle' (principle (a)) is meant to counter; of this he writes 'once we are troubled by the influence of either social contingencies or natural chance on the determination of distributive shares, we are bound, on reflection, to be bothered by the influence of the other. From a moral standpoint the two seem equally arbitrary' (1999: 64–5).

[22] Rawls (1999: 167) writes that nothing would be gained by attributing altruism to the parties in the original position, because when the ends of separate persons clash, a 'love of mankind' would need to fall back on the two principles of justice to adjudicate conflicts.

condition, and are consistent with basic liberties and fair equality of opportunity[23] (1999: 131).

In his specification of the second principle, Rawls speaks of 'the greatest expected benefit' of the least advantaged: 'We simply maximise the expectations of the least favoured subject to the required constraints' (1999: 69). A natural question would be why the maxim to improve everyone's condition should entail maximising the expectations of the least well off. Rawls acknowledges that his difference principle could be seen as unfairly biased towards the least favoured (1999: 88). However, his response is that under a Pareto-efficient arrangement in which no one's position can be improved without making another worse off, the expectations of only one social group can be maximised at any one time. This must be the least well off, because

if we give any more weight to the more fortunate, we are valuing for their own sake the gains to those already more favoured by natural and social contingencies. No one had an antecedent claim to benefited in this way, and so to maximise a weighted mean is, so to speak, to favour the more fortunate twice over. (1999: 88)

He also assumes that subject to the constraints of equal liberties and fair equality of opportunity, the distribution of income and wealth should be as close to Pareto-efficient as possible, so that no one's position can be improved if doing so would leave others unaffected.

I have given here a succinct outline of how Rawls arrives at his two principles of justice. However, what needs to be ascertained is whether the modern business corporation is an analogy to what Rawls calls the 'basic structure of society' close enough not to hinder the application of his principles. The key question in the light of the traditional theories of the social contract is whether the common purpose of mutual protection (or any other common purpose), for the sake of which the sovereign power is created in the first place, is present among all the stakeholders of a business corporation. Likewise in the case of Rawls, before one argues for the moral principles that should govern the exercise of power by the state or corporation in protecting liberties or

---

[23] This is the central idea that Freeman draws on in arguing for 'a basic moral equality among stakeholders in terms of their moral rights as these are realized in the firm, and . . . inequalities among stakeholders are justified if they raise the level of the least well-off stakeholder' (1994: 415–6).

carrying out distributive justice, one might enquire *how* these powers are first acquired.

The place of voluntary consent and the need for mutual protection in Rawls's theory have been mentioned already. However, Rawls is less clear than the other writers engaged with as to how the basic unit of social justice, 'society' itself (and its basic structure), comes to be in a position to distribute the primary social goods. Each of the other writers employs the idea of a 'State of Nature' to explain why each individual would give his or her consent to a sovereign power. However, Rawls's use of the concept does not give a possible rationale for the existence of political society bearing a sovereign power. He tells us that his concept of the 'original position' replaces the traditional idea of a 'State of Nature' (1999: 3). Yet as shown, this is used by Rawls as a means for deducing principles of justice that human beings in a state of equality would consent to *if* they were to form a society. It does *not* explain the motivation for forming a society with an exclusive power to distribute goods and protect liberties. He does allude to the Hobbesian idea of mutual protection as the central motivating factor, but his definition of 'society' would seem to cover much that goes beyond the scope of what Hobbes and other theorists had in mind when discussing sovereign power. Rawls describes 'society' as 'a cooperative venture for mutual advantage' and 'a more or less self-sufficient association of persons' (1999: 4). This would seem to cover many forms of association smaller in scale than the traditional idea of the state – for example, the extended family of a subsistence-level economy, or the small-scale commune of left libertarian theory or the networks of 'black' markets for illegal goods that flourish without any state regulation. As associations could be conceived under Rawls's definition that are *not*, as a matter of fact, formed primarily (if at all) for reasons of mutual protection and which do not have an exclusive right of physical coercion over their members, Rawls's idea of 'society' is not literally equivalent to the state as traditionally conceived. When he writes that the basic structure of society distributes certain primary goods, such as 'rights, liberties, and opportunities, and income and wealth' (1999: 54), one might ask how 'society' comes to be in control of these goods in the first place.

Rawls makes certain comments which imply that he has something like the Hobbesian conception of society in mind. Unlike Locke (1689/1988: 319), for whom different forms of society (between man and wife, parents and children, master and servant, etc.) can exist prior to the creation of 'political' society, Rawls seems to follow Hobbes's (1651/1996: 84) view that there is no form of society possible where there is no coercive power of government. This is certainly the implication of his view that a society, which he says has the coercive power necessary to protect basic liberties and distribute social goods, is 'a scheme of cooperation without which no one would have a satisfactory life' (1999: 13) and which is 'a necessary condition of the welfare of all' (1999: 13–14).

Any further discussion of the vagueness of Rawls's idea of a rationale for the formation of political society, in the light of which the tailoring of his principles of justice to fit the 'ends' of the contracting parties (I mentioned the Kantian defence of his second principle above) could also be questioned, would be fascinating to explore but is unnecessary here. What is important in assessing how Rawls's principles can be applied to the business corporation is that in keeping with the traditional theory, his contractual approach is intended to produce principles that apply at the level of the state, and not for private associations within a state. The fact that his principles of justice are meant to regulate not individual conduct but the major social institutions has already been noted. He writes that his principles 'may not work for the rules and practices of private associations or for those of less comprehensive social groups' (1999: 7) and that the subject of justice is the basic structure of society, *not* 'the rules of corporate associations' (1999: 126). For the purposes of his argument, he conceives of society as 'a closed system isolated from other societies' (1999: 7), which would seem to rule out a business corporation interacting with other associations within a state. Finally, as regards the discretion for acting on the principles of justice, he is unequivocal that this is only a concern at the level of the basic structure:

> The conduct of individuals guided by their rational plans should be coordinated as far as possible to achieve results which although *not intended or perhaps even foreseen by them* are nevertheless the best ones from the standpoint of social justice. . . . It is the aim of the ideal legislator in enacting laws and of the moralist in urging their reform. (1999: 49, emphasis added)

If the normative principles that underpin the traditional social contract theory as well as Rawls's own approach are intended to apply strictly to the coercive power of the state and not to individuals or private associations, then it may look as if the responsibilities of the business corporation cannot be captured at all by this theoretical framework. The applicability of this tradition of political theory to the business corporation depends on whether the corporation can be seen as a legal individual regulated by the sovereign power *within* a scheme of social cooperation, or as an association with sovereign power in its *own right*. The key point can be illustrated further by considering two remaining normative principles that are drawn upon, 'fairness' and 'distributive justice'. Neither relates directly to the social contract tradition, but the relevance of both to the business corporation turns out to have much in common with what has already been discussed.

Fairness and distributive justice

The crucial issue with the principles of fairness and distributive justice in the context of stakeholder theory is not their philosophical validity, though of course this is an important issue, but (as with the scope of the social contract theory) the appropriateness of their application. Two interrelated questions can be asked: first, are these principles merely constraints on the way that individuals should conduct themselves with one another, or are they principles for regulating the overall structure of society and beyond the scope of an individual's action? Second, is the corporation to be viewed as an individual constrained by the rules of the society, or is it in some sense a coercive power in its own right?

Chapter 2 argued that the problem with Phillips's (2003) theory is that his principle of 'Stakeholder Fairness' – that the voluntary acceptance of benefits creates obligations in proportion to the benefits received (2003: 91–2) – is not inconsistent with the *shareholder* theory of the firm. However, this chapter overlooks this point and asks whether the principle would suggest treating the corporation as an institution capable of determining issues of fairness between stakeholders, as a state would override the judgement of its individual citizens on judicial matters, or whether it applies to the conduct of individuals only. The next chapter argues that *if* a corporation is perceived as an individual trading on a market (or a combination of shareholders with a common interest, but with no more legal power than a single individual), then it is difficult to argue that the firm can pursue a legitimate objective other than that of shareholder interests.

Phillips (2003: 85) traces the concept of fairness back to J. S. Mill (1859/1991) and H. L. A. Hart (1955), but believes that the 'moral foundation' of stakeholder theory should be based on the principle of fair play as articulated by Rawls. To use Phillips's (2003: 87) summary of Rawls, the principle applies for a scheme of cooperation in which there is mutual benefit, the basic social institutions are just, benefits accrue only under conditions of near unanimity of cooperation, sacrifices are required on the part of participants, there is the possibility of free riders, and all the benefits are accepted voluntarily.[24] The 'duty of fair play' is then operative: 'We are not to gain from the cooperative labours of others without doing our fair share' (Rawls 1999: 96). If we look in which category Rawls places this principle in his diagram of 'practical reasoning' (1999: 94), the relevance of the principle to individuals rather than social institutions becomes clear. In the *'concept of right'* Rawls distinguishes between 'social systems and institutions' and 'individuals'. Under the moral 'requirements' of individuals (as opposed to 'permissions') he lists 'natural duties' and 'obligations', and *'fairness'* falls under the category of 'obligations'. Therefore, this principle is not thought to apply to social institutions, and he writes: 'obligations are normally owed to definite individuals, namely, those who are cooperating together to maintain the arrangement in question' (1999: 97). Indeed, in his application of the principle, Phillips (2003: 93) could not be clearer on this point. He writes that fairness-based moral obligations to stakeholders 'fill in the gaps left undetermined by the legal system' and 'While the legal system dictates much about stakeholder relations, there is still much left to the moral discretion of managers and administrators.' The concept of fairness, whether or not it is applied to the corporation, does not appear in these authors to have any relation to the 'basic structure' of society, and would seem to fall outside the context of the contractual tradition altogether.

With the remaining normative principle, that of 'distributive justice', it is possible to see two particular approaches taken in stakeholder theory. Many theorists draw on Rawls's theory of justice. As seen earlier, a

---

[24] These are the conditions listed by Rawls (1999). However, Phillips (2003: 87–90) argues convincingly that the conditions of 'justice' and 'unanimity of cooperation' are unnecessary for obligations of fairness to arise at the organisational level.

part of Rawls's second principle – that economic inequalities be arranged to the greatest expected benefit of the least well off – is an argument for distributing the wealth of society. However, as also seen above, this principle for Rawls is meant to apply to the arrangement of the basic structure, and not to how individuals within the structure act towards each other. This would again raise the question of whether the corporation can be seen as a basic social structure in its own right, or whether it has no more political power than a private individual.

The same issue arises with the other, non-Rawlsian, approach to distributive justice. When Donaldson and Preston (1995: 83–4) argue that the source of property rights must lie in the claims of distributive justice, such as need, ability and effort, they draw on a number of recent theorists of property. One authority they cite is Stephen Munzer's (1990) *A Theory of Property*, which (amongst other issues) analyses the responsibility of the corporation through the lens of three different principles of distributive justice – utility and efficiency, labour desert, and justice and equality. Munzer appears to come to conclusions that would support a stakeholder view of the firm: for example, from the principle of *desert*, he argues for (1) a defensible wage policy; (2) seeing work as a social activity for self-esteem and self-respect of employees, so that they should have some control over the work place; and (3) a worker's property right over his job, secured by effort, persistence, time spent on the job, responsibility, etc. (1990: 346).

However, when Munzer discusses how such principles would be implemented, he comes to conclusions that are similar to Rawls's institution-level theory of distribution. He writes that in the case of 'justice and equality' no single corporation can affect the equality of wealth in a society in such a way as to undermine the general quality of life (1990: 349). Accordingly, constraints on corporations must be *system-wide* rather than applying at the particular level of individual corporations (1990: 350). Furthermore, for the principle of utility/efficiency, because the preference satisfactions of *all* are relevant, governments should step in to regulate corporations to prevent externalities; and for the labour desert principle, governments may require corporations to pay a minimum wage and to enhance employee participation (1990: 351). The emphasis is very much on *governments* taking responsibility for meeting the demands of distributive justice, unlike the principle of fairness, which is the concern only of individuals and corporations as *private* associations.

Regarding the relevance of both these principles for the stakeholder theory of the firm, two particular points can be made. First, whether one appeals to the fairness principle as a moral constraint on the conduct of individuals, or distributive justice as a guide for the legal framework in which companies operate, one is still left with a situation compatible with the shareholder objective. Whether the constraints are legal or moral, managers could still run the firm with the objective of maximising shareholder wealth subject to these constraints. Second, the conditions under which these principles would *replace* the objective of the firm would arise, in the case of distributive justice, if the firm *itself* was to take on the role of regulating the distribution of its profits (with the power to override contractual exchanges with stakeholders) instead of leaving this to the legal framework. The corporation would be, in relation to its stakeholders, a sovereign power in its own right. The question of whether the principle of 'fairness' could support a stakeholder theory of the firm depends on whether a moral principle attached to the actions of a private association (or individual) can support a corporate objective separate from that of shareholder interests.

Conclusion

This chapter has given a detailed account of the philosophical traditions within which the normative stakeholder arguments are situated. In the work of Rawls, the social contract tradition, and the work on distributive justice by Munzer (1990), the ethical principles established clearly apply to the overall structure of a society or state, which in turn possesses exclusive power to regulate the property of its subjects. It is said that the extent of sovereign power cannot exceed the assumed *consent* of all who are subject to it, and that the power exists on the basis of a common purpose (e.g., mutual protection) to which all give their consent. As all are considered equal in this respect, the *rule of law* as exercised by a single judicial authority is a necessary criterion for the legitimate exercise of this power. If stakeholder theory is to draw on this branch of philosophy to make the case for a stakeholder objective, it must be shown how the modern corporation approximates these characteristics of sovereign power. What is the common purpose that commands the voluntary consent of all stakeholders? Can the corporation put into practice a set of rules, publicly declared, that deal with all stakeholders equally? In what sense does it have exclusive judicial authority over the claims of its stakeholders to the corporation's wealth? These questions are considered later in Chapter 5.

The concept of *fairness* appears to differ from the other normative principles, as it has been theorised at the level of the individual or private association of individuals rather than the state or 'social structure'. While in the case of Phillips's (2003) use of the concept it is unclear how it might replace the shareholder objective, the more important question is whether a moral principle which applies only to individuals can be used to displace the shareholder view of the firm. In other words, does the corporation have to be viewed as a public institution rather than as a private entity (composed of individuals whose interests do not constitute 'sovereign power'), if the corporation is to be run in the interests of stakeholders? Are the principles that apply to the state as understood in social contract theory the only principles relevant in assessing stakeholder theory? Before any similarity between the concept of the state and that of the corporation is addressed, it should first be asked if the corporation as a *private* entity is compatible with the stakeholder view.

4 | *The corporation as a private association in a market economy*

Chapter 3 raised the problem of whether the corporation should be viewed, for the purposes of stakeholder theory, as a public entity with sovereign power over its stakeholders or simply as a private association. In deciding if either conception provides an adequate basis for stakeholder theory, a normative *context* needs to be established in terms of which these conceptions can be evaluated. This necessarily involves the moral context in which the business corporation operates: a context logically prior to an appeal to the principles of fairness, distributive justice, etc., as a support for particular versions of the theory. It is here that a *market economy* and the ethical framework this implies (accepted, as seen in Chapter 1, by the majority of stakeholder theorists) become relevant. If one of these concepts of the corporation is assumed as a premise for deducing corporate responsibilities, it must be seen that such a conception is consistent with a stakeholder objective in a market economy. This requires an examination of the ethical principles that should be observed collectively in a society for which market exchange is legitimate.[1] An analysis of the corporate objective in this context can then be carried out.

Starting from the assumption that what is essential to any concept of a market economy is the activity of trade itself, I begin by asking what is

---

[1] It might be objected that there is scarcely to be found anywhere a society in which *all* income is generated through market exchange, so it is misleading to deduce ethical principles that apply strictly to the market, and say that these would be observed throughout a 'market economy'. However, in line with the epistemological position given in Chapter 1, ethical principles are treated here as objective properties which to the observer appear universal. Therefore, if a unanimous decision was taken in a society to organise only 10% of its economy around the market, the ethical reasoning it would accept in granting moral legitimacy to market exchange (in however restricted a form) would be experienced as universally binding on all in that society, even if it found other (nonconflicting) principles on which to base an organisation of the rest of the economy on public ownership.

essential to the concept of trade. Instead of attempting an exhaustive account of everything that might fall under the concept, I look at the minimal criteria (in terms of the subjective dispositions of the individual actors involved) that must be present for the activity of trade to occur. Although there are of course different types of market, and existing market economies differ in many of their empirical features, the important issue is what is essential to *any* act of trade. This means studying what trade entails *inherently*, rather than what is observed contingently in the different forms of trade that occur in practice.

An analysis of the concept of trade

It can be said that if stakeholder theorists claim consistency between their approach and a market economy, then an analysis of stakeholder theory can assume that a basic act of trade between two or more people is morally permissible, ceteris paribus. That is to say, the actions that would by themselves constitute a basic act of trade (as I attempt to define it) are not in violation of any ethical constraints a priori. Of course, the content of trade, which may include the sale of arms, illicit drugs, slaves, etc., may violate ethical constraints. However, it is assumed that the general concept of trade itself is not, in a market economy, taken to imply anything unethical.

The understanding of trade, or market exchange, offered here is that it constitutes a form of human action. It is not an end in itself, or the realisation of a particular purpose or view of the good. It is an instrumental form of action, a means to the satisfaction of some of the purposes or goals of the individual who engages in trade. The content of the ends pursued through trade is left undetermined by the concept, except for the fact that in the perception of the individuals engaged in it, the ends are such that they are (at least in part) achievable through this form of action. From this understanding of trade as a means for satisfying individual expectations, the assumption of *rationality* can be seen as a key part of the concept. By rationality I refer to the capacity of an individual to conceive a specific goal or purpose of his or her action, and to make a judgement (however temporary) as to what actions will be most effective in achieving this goal.[2]

---

[2] Rationality as I use the term could be described as 'bounded rationality', which does not imply full information about the choices available. This concept of

To be more precise, in emphasising the rational expectations of persons that their actions will achieve particular results, what is entailed is the conscious direction of external objects for the satisfaction of personal ends. By *ends* I refer simply to the aims, purposes or goals to which a person consciously directs their action. Of course, this part of the concept so far discussed is incomplete, as no recognition has been made of the *interpersonal* aspect of trade. Each of the elements hitherto described could apply to the actions of an isolated individual acting on the environment to satisfy his or her needs, without requiring interaction with another person. The reciprocal nature of trade should therefore be encompassed in this analysis.

A first step to recognising the interpersonal aspect of trade would be simply to posit the existence of at least two individual subjects as an essential part of the concept. This seemingly obvious move would provide a needed qualification to the view of individual rationality given above. However, what remains to be emphasised is the *complementary* relationship between individual rationality and the existence of separate subjects with respect to trade. The conditions for the realisation of individual ends through the activity of trade are now explored.

It can be assumed that trade as a rational device for satisfying the ends of a plurality of individuals is possible under the following necessary condition. A minimum of two individuals must value at least two distinct objects as a means for satisfying their personal ends, and there must be an inequality in the value attached to the two objects in the mind of each individual. This can be called an inequality in 'subjective value'. It follows that if an individual is indifferent between the two distinct objects, there would be no reason to trade one for the other. Furthermore, the difference in subjective value, for the individual concerned, must be in some way quantifiable. So there must be a certain quantity of one good (by which is meant a valued object) that leaves the person indifferent between that and the other good. For example, if the two goods in question were a life-saving treatment for a person terminally ill and a pint of beer, it is unlikely there would be a quantity of beer at which the person would be indifferent between

rationality does not contradict the existence of speculative market 'bubbles', which arise because of the lack of complete information about the present value of underlying commodities.

the two. For the terminally ill patient, not only are the two goods of different subjective value, but also the difference is not *quantifiable*. If the subjective value *can* be quantified, as between a glass of wine and a pint of beer, for example, then a condition for trade is fulfilled.

A further condition is that for two individuals who each have a subjective value for two goods, the *ratios* between these two values must differ. If one individual possesses a pint of beer and the other a glass of wine, and yet the beer and wine are of *equal* value to both, there will be no incentive to trade. One could not give the other anything that is more valuable in realising his or her ends than what they already possess. It should be noted that although a condition of trade is that two individuals have different ratios of subjective values for two distinct objects, it is *not* necessary for them to have a different value for each object considered separately. For example, in an economy based on money, which Marx (1867/1995: 58)[3] calls a 'universal measure of value', two individuals may value one unit of the currency equally, but value several goods differently with respect to that unit. As long as the ratios of value for the same goods are different between two individuals, then if both are in possession of one of the goods in question, trade can take place.

The concept of *possession* will be explored in the next section. For now it can be assumed that possession simply implies the control of an object. If each of these conditions is fulfilled, so that at least two individuals are each in possession of an object distinct from the object possessed by the other, with each of the objects being a *good* to each individual (i.e., perceived as possessing properties capable of satisfying their ends), and the ratios of value for the two objects differ between the two individuals, then there is both the incentive and the possibility for trade to occur. These can be taken as the minimal conditions of trade.

---

[3] Marx, in the first volume of *Capital* (1867/1976), writes: 'The first chief function of money is to supply commodities with the material for the expression of their values, or to represent their values as magnitudes of the same denomination, qualitatively equal, and quantitatively comparable. It thus serves as a *universal measure of value*' (1867/1995: 58, emphasis in original). Marx's labour theory of value aside, this brief account of money (which Marx goes on to expound in Chapter 3 of Volume One) serves adequately for this analysis.

It follows that a *price* agreed on between two persons trading goods can never be equal to either person's subjective ratio of value for the two goods. Imagine, for example, that person A is indifferent between a glass of wine and £3, and person B is indifferent between the same glass and £5. Let us add that person A is in possession of the glass of wine and person B is in possession of £5. If the wine and pound sterling are valued by both persons, then it is rational ceteris paribus for trade to take place between A and B. However, the price at which the trade is made will not be either £3 or £5, but anything from £3.01 up to £4.99,[4] a range in which any point is subjectively profitable for both persons.[5] This has an implication for the popular criticism of so-called 'neo-liberal' free market discourses: that all value is reduced to 'market value'. For example, Jones et al. (2005: 109), following Marx (1847/1955: 30), write that 'in capitalist societies, the value of all things tends to become nothing more than what one pays for them'. However, it would seem a contradiction for all subjective values to be *equal* to market value, for then there would be no market. The *differences* in the subjective value that persons have for the same goods provide the necessary incentive for trade.

It should also be emphasised that in seeking to explain how trade can yield a subjective profit for all parties to an exchange, there is no assumption of a 'zero-sum' view of competition in which a dominant group emerges to 'capture' value created by others (cf. Freeman et al., 2010: 276). In other words, this section explores the *cooperative* conditions for value creation, and is consistent with Freeman et al.'s (2010: 281) 'principle of stakeholder cooperation': 'Value can be created, traded, and sustained because stakeholders can jointly satisfy their needs and desires by making voluntary agreements with each other that for the most part are kept'.

This analysis of the concept of trade will suffice as an outline of the form of economic activity which is essential to a market economy. If a market economy is a morally acceptable form of economic

---

[4] By taking exchange value to be based on subjective values, I am working without the assumption of an objective determinant of value common to 'classical' economists such as Smith, Ricardo and Marx.

[5] The term *subjective profit* refers here to the quantity of a good that a person gains above the level at which he or she would have been indifferent between that good and another.

organisation – a view receiving explicit support from many stakeholder theorists – then the outline given here must by implication be approved also. If the concept of trade is inherently ethical, then it can now be asked which principles serve as a sufficient basis for it.

The ethical principles of a market economy

It can be argued that there are at least two principles that are implied if the concept of trade outlined above is morally acceptable. This is not to imply that all market exchange is necessarily ethical, but only that it would be inconsistent to deny these principles while accepting the legitimacy of a capitalist economy. The first is an individual right to the ownership of external objects, which can be called *property*, and a corresponding duty to respect this right in others.[6] The second principle can be derived from the same source as the first,[7] and is the right to the future performance of another's action, if the expectation of this action is created with the consent of both parties. Again there is a corresponding duty to respect this right in others. This second principle involves the rights and duties of entering a *contract*.[8]

An objection might be raised to the emphasis being placed on the necessary principles of a market economy, which should be answered before an elucidation of these principles is carried out. It could be said that although stakeholder theorists have proclaimed the consistency of their approach with a market economy, one cannot infer the

---

[6] Both Jones (1994: 15) and Becker (1977: 21) suggest that a right to property is a *claim-right*, which implies the right not to be interfered with, and the corresponding duty for all others to observe this.

[7] With the exception, according to Jones (1994: 15), that whereas a property right is a 'negative' claim-right not to be interfered with by people at large (*in rem*), a contractual right is a 'positive' claim-right to specific things from individual people (*in personam*).

[8] One could ask if these rights take the form of inviolable side-constraints or merely *derivative* rights which can be overridden by higher moral principles. For example, as Becker (1977: 35) points out, John Locke's famous defence of property rights is derived from an absolute right to the ownership of one's body, and could therefore be overridden if it clashed with this prior right. In the case of the rights discussed here, it is impossible to say whether they are derivative or absolute, as the intention is merely to show their logical entailment if the concept of trade is ethical. Whether rights of property, contract and exchange would have an absolute status in an overall theory of rights is an open question; the concern here is to point to the logical relations between them.

acceptance of any underlying moral principles that must apply in such an economy. Perhaps stakeholder theorists advocate a market economy because this serves an instrumental purpose of bringing about desirable social goals, such as the alleviation of poverty, an equitable distribution of wealth, or equality of opportunity. If other economic arrangements would serve these aims more effectively then there would be no reason to cling to a fundamental ethic of the market. Kaler (2006: 253–4), for example, claims that managers should have the power to override shareholder property rights on grounds of 'public interest', using the example of people being forced to make way for construction and development by selling their homes.

The response would simply be that stakeholder theorists mostly accept a concept of the firm that is based on market contracts. In stating the evidence for this view it should be noted that a systematic rejection of the contractual view is attempted by John Boatright (1994), though he is perhaps the only advocate of stakeholder theory to do so. He writes that even if it is granted that shareholders own the firm's assets, there is a 'logical gap' between this ownership and management having a duty to run the firm solely in shareholder interests (1994: 395). Boatright argues that there is no express contract between managers and shareholders, nor even an implied contract, because most shareholders buy their shares from other shareholders rather than from the corporation itself and there is a lack of face-to-face dealings between the two parties (1994: 397–8). Boatright (1994: 398) also rules out a 'social contract' because of the lack of negotiating space between management and shareholders. His conclusion is that there is no agency relation between managers and shareholders, and the law gives management a fiduciary responsibility to shareholders only on grounds of 'public policy' (1994: 400).

However, Boatright's (1994) rejection of the contractual view is not taken up consistently by defenders of stakeholder theory. Donaldson and Preston state that many business relationships are formed other than through contracts, such as relationships with communities which are too vague to be considered as a contract, and therefore 'We believe that the firm-as-contract perspective, *although correct*, is incomplete as a description of the corporation' (1995: 85, emphasis added). Freeman (1994: 415) is somewhat ambiguous on the matter, first denying that the firm is 'the result of a voluntary contracting process' because this would separate ethics from business, and then proposing that we understand the value-creating activity of the firm 'as a contractual process among those parties affected' (ibid.). Again, according to Freeman and Evan's (1990: 342) argument for representation on the board of directors for parties whose asset-specific investments are at risk: 'Voting membership by parties to a contract is, in spirit at least, quite consistent with the contract view of the firm. The chief purpose of the firm, on this view, is to efficiently administer the contracts with its stakeholders.' They specifically discuss the *contract* between shareholders and management (1990: 340). Moreover, Freeman and Phillips (2002: 338) hold that corporate obligations are created through contracts reached by voluntary consent, which they claim is consistent with seeing the firm as a nexus of contracts.

If a contractual view of the firm is shared by the majority of leading writers on stakeholder theory, then although by a consequentialist line of reasoning exceptions could be made to the ethical principles that underpin a market economy (e.g., if public policies employing nonmarket solutions could generate desirable consequences more effectively than the market), the *corporation* is for stakeholder theorists no such exception. As they hold the corporation to be a creation of market contracts and not a publicly controlled organisation (although it may have purposes of its own analogous to those of a state, as explored in Chapter 5), it seems valid to assess the normative arguments for stakeholder theory on the basis of the ethical principles that are consistent with any market economy. Such an approach is consistent with the 'stakeholder capitalism' of Freeman et al. (2010: 280): 'we do not need to justify capitalistic systems based on the outcome or the alternatives – the principles of capitalism are worthy goals in and of themselves'.

The ethical principles that follow logically from the concept of trade can now be derived. The first is an individual right to the ownership of *property*. As argued above, trade can be understood as an inherently *rational* activity which takes place in accordance with individuals' desires to satisfy their ends. Clearly, this is rational for a given individual only if he or she believes that at least a part of these ends can be satisfied through trade. It follows that if the activity of trade is morally acceptable, then an individual can claim a moral right to the ownership of the fruits of trade. Following Becker (1977: 19), it can be said that 'the right to the capital' – 'the power to alienate the thing and to consume, waste, modify, or destroy it' – is sufficient for ownership of an object to exist.[9] Therefore, if an individual cannot exclude others from the right to the capital that he or she gains, there is no way trade can play a part in his or her plans as a means of satisfying an end, and trade cannot be a rational activity at all. Ownership therefore implies the right to exclude others, by force if necessary, from the control or use of an object gained through trade.

Kant (1797/1996), in *The Metaphysics of Morals*, provides a useful conceptual distinction between rightful ownership and the empirical possession of a good. Kant (1797/1996: 37) writes that the 'merely rightful' (though not empirical) possession of an object is *intelligible* possession. According to Kant, this means that I cannot call an object mine unless, '*even though I am not in physical possession of it*, I can still assert that I am actually in some other (hence not physical) possession of it' (1797/1996: 38, emphasis in original). The idea is that ownership of property is not conditional upon one's relation to an object in time and space – involving, for example, the ability to exercise immediate control over it – but is entirely an *intelligible* relation. One has the right to determine how property is used even if one is not in immediate possession of it.

It has been argued that trade depends on the rational expectation that a given object will satisfy a given need. As this is necessarily a future expectation before the trade occurs, the transfer of property must take place in accordance with an expression of one's will. In turn, this cannot depend on one's future empirical circumstances. If I buy a house but on the day the house is transferred to my name I am taken ill, and while in hospital cannot physically occupy the house, it does not follow that I cannot call the house my own until I recover.

It can be observed that this link between the expectation that an object will satisfy a need and the right to own that object if acquired through trade is consistent with John Locke's (1689/1988) theory of property rights in *The Second Treatise of Government*. As Locke puts it, before a fruit or venison can nourish anyone it must be *his*, if it is to do him any good and support his life (1689/1988: 287). He emphasises that for an object to be used with the conscious intention of benefiting ourselves from it, such as in the consumption of food to sustain ourselves, we must first *own* the benefits that we are procuring. Only

[9] Becker (1977) is working with Honoré's (1961) criteria for what constitutes 'full ownership' of an object.

under this principle of natural right, Locke argues, can mankind appropriate from the world the advantages of life and convenience for its own benefit (1689/1988: 286–7). Murray Rothbard (1982) builds directly on Locke's individualist methodology (1982: 21) and theory of property rights (1982: 34)[10] to argue that the notion of ownership (understood in Locke's sense) is implied in the very concept of exchange:

> But economists too often forget, in contemplating the critical importance and the glories of the free market, *what* precisely is being exchanged. For apples are *not* simply being exchanged for butter, or gold for horses. What is really being exchanged is not the commodities themselves, but the *rights to ownership* of them.[11] When Smith exchanges a bag of apples for Jones's pound of butter, he is actually transferring his *ownership rights* in the apples for the ownership rights to the butter, and vice versa. (1982: 36, emphases in original)

These arguments present a valid case for seeing a right to the ownership of individual property as implied in the concept of trade, assuming that the concept itself does not contradict any ethical constraints a priori. As stakeholder theorists accept the framework of a market economy as part of the context in which business operates, this assumption continues to be made.

However, an important line of argument for property rights has been missing from this discussion. So far it has been argued that the notion of ownership arises logically if the concept of trade is considered morally legitimate. The most that can be defended here is a property right that arises directly *from trade*. However, one could argue that a property right can be created from the first acquisition of an object (e.g., when a valuable item is discovered such as an oasis in a desert), or through production and the application of labour to make an object valuable in the first place. Locke (1689/1988: 296) argues that "tis *Labour* indeed that *puts the difference of value* on every

---

[10] See Locke (1689/1988: 285–302) for the corresponding section of his argument.

[11] Rothbard's (1982: 36) contention that commodities themselves are not exchanged, but ownership rights to them, seems to resonate with Kant's (1797/1996: 49–54) theory of property rights. Kant points out that speaking literally there is never a *direct* right to a thing, but only a right against *other persons* who would have had an equal right of ownership before the thing was originally acquired (1797/1996: 50).

thing'[12] (emphases in original) and that whatsoever a man removes from the 'State of Nature' 'he hath mixed his *Labour* with, and joined to it something that is his own, and thereby makes it his *Property* . . . it hath by this *labour* something annexed to it, that excludes the common right of other Men' (1689/1988: 288, emphases in original). Furthermore, Rothbard (1982) asserts that the link between ownership and exchange is intelligible only in the context of *production*. He writes:

Ownership rights are acquired in two ways and two ways only: (a) by finding and transforming resources ('producing'), and (b) by exchanging one's produce for someone else's product – including the medium of exchange, or 'money' commodity. And it is clear that method (b) *reduces* logically to (a), for the only way a person can obtain something in exchange is by giving up his own product. In short there is only one route to ownership of goods: production-and-exchange. (1982: 37, emphasis in original)

Taking these arguments into consideration, a more complete account of property rights could be derived. However, no more importance will be attached to these points here, because the ethical principles being derived must be strictly consistent with the concept of trade and a market economy. This is so that the argument remains within a framework valid for the criticism of stakeholder theory, and the only premises that can be assumed are those consistent with the stakeholder theory literature.

The second ethical principle that can be seen as fundamental to a market economy is the right of *contract*. This can be derived in much the same manner as the first, if instead of the rational expectation that an object of trade will satisfy an *individual's* purposes, the interpersonal aspect is brought into focus. For if trade is based on a rational expectation that its gains will satisfy a person's ends, and trade is necessarily *interpersonal*, in that the fulfilment of one person's expectations is bound to the performance of specific actions by another, then if trade itself is moral there must be a right to the enforcement of these actions. In other words, there exists a right to the enforcement of

---

[12] Although not using this insight as a basis for natural rights, Marx in *Capital* also holds that a commodity has a use-value only because of the labour power expended upon it. He writes: 'A use-value, or useful article . . . has value only because human labour in the abstract has been embodied or materialised in it' (1867/1995: 16).

contracts.[13] Of course, there are manifold difficulties in determining the existence of a contract and the extent to which it is enforceable. Socrates famously asks in the first book of the *Republic* whether it is always right to return to friends what is owed, and doubts this with the example of a weapon borrowed from a friend who later loses his sanity (Plato 1994: 8). There are also many difficulties in determining the existence of consent (and the difference between 'express' and 'tacit' consent) in reaching contractual agreements.

Nonetheless, the way a contract is understood here is that consent to the future performance of an action (i.e., to the transfer of property) must always be present, however difficult its presence may be to determine in practice. This understanding is close to that of Kant (1797/1996: 57), for whom a contract right is a system of laws in accordance with which I possess another's choice. Kant (1797/1996: 59) observes that by a contract one acquires not an external thing but rather the *deed* of another: 'Hence the right that arises from a contract is only a right against a person, and becomes a right to a *thing* only by delivery of that thing' (1797/1996: 60, emphasis in original). From Kant's position a specific grasp can be gained of the place of *consent* in the concept of contract. It can be said that the basis of a contract is the *will* of each contracting party. In other words, the expectation that the other's actions will be consistent with the will of the contracting parties is what is decisive in the *moral* (if not always legal) enforceability of the other's actions. Kant (1797: 58) argues that a contract is not concluded by the separate will of either contractor, but by the *united will* of both: 'An act of the united choice of two persons by which anything at all that belongs to one passes to the other is a *contract*' (1797/1996: 57, emphasis in original).

What counts as an adequate expression of an individual's will, such that his or her rational expectations are known to the person with whom he or she is contracting, is difficult to determine. However, it is worth reflecting on attempts that have been made. For Hobbes (1651/1996: 89), signs of contract are either *express* or by *inference*.

---

[13] Rothbard (1982: 133) puts the relationship between property and contracts succinctly: 'the right to contract is strictly derivable from the right of private property . . . the only *enforceable* contracts (i.e., those backed by the sanction of legal coercion) should be those where the failure of one party to abide by the contract implies the *theft* of property from the other party' (emphases in original).

Express signs 'are words spoken with understanding of what they signify'. Signs by inference can be from the consequence of words, the consequence of silence, consequence of actions, or forbearing an action, or 'whatsoever sufficiently argues the will of the contractor' (ibid.). Hobbes's point supports what has been said already insofar as some act of will is necessary in any form of consent.

By contrast, in Locke's account of 'tacit' consent, the existence of a voluntary act of will is conspicuously absent. He asks what can be understood as a sufficient declaration of a man's consent to make him subject to the laws of a government (1689/1988: 347). While *express* consent clearly does bind, he asks how we are to recognise *tacit* consent, and how far it binds? He answers: 'every Man, that hath any Possession, or Enjoyment, of any part of the Dominions of any Government, doth thereby give his *tacit Consent*' (1689/1988: 348, emphasis in original). However, without an explicit or voluntary act of will, this is difficult to accept as a form of consent. A person may have property stolen and deposited under a foreign government without his/her knowledge, or may involuntarily receive benefits such as hearing a virtuoso street musician while passing by. In neither of these situations is it obvious that a person would be consenting to the laws of the government or anything else. Moreover, it seems that what counts as a benefit or 'enjoyment' for me cannot be *known* to anyone else without a voluntary act of approval on my part (what if I dislike the street musician's playing?). Robert Phillips (1997, 2003), while not mentioning Locke, has rightly questioned whether the mere receipt of benefits implies anything about consent.

My understanding of the right of contract supposes the expression of a voluntary act of will as a sign of consent. The right to enforce a contract must stem from the consent of both parties to fulfil the mutual expectations present in the acts of will that constitute the contract. Again, it can be noted that the principles defended here are broadly consistent with those proposed by Freeman et al. (2010: 280) as a basis for 'stakeholder capitalism': 'First adults have *freedom* to do what they want, including making voluntary agreements that are sustainable over time ... Second, individuals have *rights* protecting them in those agreements ... each stakeholder should be protected within their voluntary agreements. Finally, those individuals can decide to cooperate and *obligate themselves* to others through those voluntary agreements' (emphases in original).

Having given what I hope is a satisfactory (if not exhaustive) outline of the minimal ethical framework of a market economy, I now apply these principles to the corporate objective. The intention is to assess whether the corporation, created as a legal individual and legitimately possessing no more coercive power than a private person, can pursue an objective other than that of shareholder wealth. Having set out the ethical principles which are fundamental to any conception of market exchange, I can now offer an answer to this question.

The corporate objective in a market economy

The analysis therefore starts with a view of the corporation as a legal individual, created for commercial purposes, which can own and trade property in its own right. This view is consistent with much of contemporary company law. In the context of UK law, Dine and Koutsias (2007: 2) write that the company as a 'fictional "legal person" owns the property of the business, owes the money that is due to business creditors and is unchanging even though the people involved come and go'. Williston (1888: 106) points out that the origin of the business corporation as a legal person separate from its members goes back to the Romans, or even perhaps to the ancient Greeks. In Roman law all sorts of groups of people were regarded as 'corporations' with separate legal identities, and a Roman business corporation 'could hold and deal with property, enjoy *usufructus*, incur obligations' (1888: 107). Furthermore, 'the conception of the corporation as a legal person, a conception going back farther than can be definitely traced, involves necessarily the consequence that before the law the corporation shall be treated like any other person' (1888: 117). Moving forward in time, Evans (1908: 340) lists some of the powers of the earliest chartered corporations of the sixteenth and seventeenth centuries: 'It could sue and be sued by its corporate name, and under and in that name it had perpetual succession, with the power to hold property, a common seal ... and so on'.

According to Dine and Koutsias (2007), this is basically the view taken in UK company law today, with the most widely discussed example in case law being that of *Salomon* v. *Salomon* [1897]. That the business corporation can be seen as a legal individual with a right to trade and own property, and which is created specifically for commercial purposes, is suggested by contemporary law and legal history.

However, the picture is complicated by the fact that the earliest civil corporations, both in Roman law and medieval England, were created to oversee the protection and security of their members, a business corporation having the legal power to regulate the trade that formed the common basis of its association[14] (Williston, 1888). Williston (1888: 110) writes that in the case of the first business corporations chartered for foreign trade in the sixteenth century (prior to the idea of joint stock funding): 'the corporation was far from being regarded as simply an organization for the more convenient prosecution of business. It was looked on as a public agency, to which had been confided the due regulation of foreign trade, just as the domestic trades were subject to the government of the guilds'.

Trading ventures to various destinations (early examples include Africa, Russia, Turkey, the East Indies and Greenland) were limited to members of the various corporations, and while the members traded on their own account and kept their own profits, the corporation itself existed in a purely regulatory capacity. Williston (1888: 110) cites a book of anonymous authorship called *The Law of Corporations* (1702) in which it is unequivocally held that the purpose of all civil corporations is *better government* rather than commercial enterprise. Even with the growth of joint stock corporations in the seventeenth century, a necessary condition in granting charters for incorporation was 'the public interest in having the undertaking prosecuted' (Williston 1888: 111).

Historians record a gradual change in the perception of the corporation as a regulatory body created for public benefit, to the corporation as a vehicle for commercial purposes in its own right. Williston gives the following account:

A few of the earlier joint-stock companies were entrusted with the regulation of the trade in which they were engaged, and the by-laws of these were binding on all engaged in the trade . . . But by the change in the conception of a corporation from an institution for special government to a simple instrumentality for carrying on a large business, the right to pass by-laws was restricted to regulations for the management of the corporate business. (1888: 122–3)

---

[14] According to Williston (1888: 107–8), the other form of civil corporation, which formed the earliest corporate associations in England, was the municipal peace guild: 'the members of which were pledged to stand by each other for mutual protection'.

However, following the statutory restrictions placed on the incorporation of companies by the 'Bubble Act' of 1720 (which was not repealed until 1825), corporations in the early nineteenth century were still associated with the trade monopolies given to the chartered corporations of two centuries before (Hunt 1935: 17). The perception that the public might benefit from *competition* between corporations and that the corporation would not undermine a system of free trade did not become familiar until the legality of the numerous joint-stock corporations formed in the post-Napoleonic war boom of 1824–5 was brought into question and the merits of corporate competition reconsidered, prior to the repeal of the 'Bubble Act'.

As the nineteenth century progressed, and with the legal status of limited liability widely available after 1855, the corporation became generally perceived as a market-based entity existing for commercial purposes rather than in its former role as an economic monopoly with regulatory power over a trade. Indeed, Alborn (1998: 7) writes that the Bank of England in the nineteenth century survived nationalisation by refashioning itself as a 'modern company', interpreted to mean that its ends should be primarily *economic* rather than political. It is safe to say that in an empirical (if not in a moral) sense the view of corporations as existing for commercial purposes is today widespread. Dine and Koutsias (2007: 68), again from a legal perspective, discuss what is meant by the phrase '*Bona fide* for the benefit of the company'[15] and write of 'the company's separate existence [from its shareholders] as a *commercial* entity in need of further funding' (emphasis added).

This is not to say that corporations since the mid-nineteenth century have carried no public obligations, or that today corporations ought not to pursue any purposes that are not strictly commercial.[16] Nor is it to imply that a corporation is restricted to forming *exclusively* commercial relationships with stakeholders. The important point is that most of the groups considered to be primary stakeholders of a corporation (customers, employees, suppliers, customers, etc.) have 'stakes' that essentially are, at least in part, based on market transactions. A company that had entirely non-commercial relationships with its

---

[15] Under UK law, this is the necessary condition for changing the articles of association of a corporation.

[16] See Crane et al. (2008) for an extensive and discerning account of the governance of citizenship by corporations.

stakeholders would not be a business corporation according to the modern understanding of the concept. The implications for the argument will soon be apparent.

If through a contract a corporation is created as a legal individual that can own and trade property, and by definition it cannot own property before it is created, then in its inception an association of property holders (if there is more than one shareholder) combine property for the pursuit of mutual interests. The property passes from their personal ownership into the legal ownership of the corporation. For the corporate objective to be ethical, the use of the corporation's assets should not contradict the property and contract rights of the first investors. The purposes of the corporation must therefore be underpinned by the joint interests either of these original property holders or of future investors who gain legal rights equivalent to those of the first investors.[17] The question that arises is whether the interests represented by the corporation are necessarily *restricted* to the ends of its shareholders. Can the association of property holders comprise other stakeholder groups? If one can answer this question then one can know which group(s) of interests cannot be contrary to the corporate objective.

In answering this question, the first consideration is the implications of the corporation being set up as a legal owner of property for commercial purposes. If the corporation engages in market exchange as an individual holder of private property, then it can be thought of as being in the position of the subject in the concept of trade outlined previously. It was argued that a moral condition for the existence of trade as a rational activity was that two or more subjects have property rights to the goods they trade. Furthermore, these rights must be *separate* if both parties are to benefit from the exchange. If two separate persons envisage an act of trade with each other as the most efficient means of satisfying their individual goals, it makes sense that the rights they have to their own property are *distinct*. If this were not the case, the goals they could pursue through trade would not be individual goals. As suggested earlier, that two people have different subjective values for the same good is a necessary condition of trade.

---

[17] Future investors who wish to alter the objectives of the corporation may of course face legal restrictions; for example, a memorandum of association which, prior to the Companies Act 2006, constrained the activities of UK companies. This point is considered further in Chapter 6.

It follows that the property rights of the persons whose interests are represented in the corporate objective cannot be those of any stakeholder with whom the corporation trades. For the corporation to exchange money for the goods of suppliers, the credit of banks, or the labour time of employees (for example), the property rights of each of these groups must be separate from the legal property right of the corporation. If the property that the corporation owns was invested in it by an employee or supplier, for example (and *not* in the role of a shareholder), then as that stakeholder enters into market exchange with the corporation, the property he or she invested could not be used in pursuit of their interests. There would then be an irrational conflict of interests. How would the corporation represent the stakeholder's interests at the same time as bargaining with that stakeholder over the price of the good to be exchanged? Two subjective values for the same good would not exist because the property being traded would already belong to the parties on both sides of the exchange. The trade itself would be a conceptual impossibility.

The property of which the corporation is the legal owner therefore cannot be invested in it by any stakeholder with whom it enters into exchange. The property rights of the corporation and those who contract with it must be distinguishable. This means that the association of property holders whose interests the corporate objective cannot contradict excludes just about every stakeholder except the shareholders. As Dine and Koutsias (2007: 23) point out, in UK law, management is obliged to act 'in the best interests of the company', and these interests are assumed to be those represented by the memorandum of association that marks the birth of the corporation as a legal individual. Under Section 7 of the Companies Act 2006, a corporation is created when one or more persons subscribe their names to a memorandum of association, and this is done by no stakeholder group other than the shareholders. For this reason, all persons other than shareholders are considered 'outsiders' in company law, which means: 'a person unable to enforce the articles [of association] or be affected by the contract in the articles' (Dine and Koutsias, 2007: 63).

From another perspective – that of the position of management as agents of the corporation – it can be seen that in using corporate property in pursuit of corporate objectives the interests of no group other than the shareholders can be represented. Dine and Koutsias (2007: 7) remark: 'directors must understand that, when they are dealing with corporate property, they are dealing with the property of the company rather than their personal property' and they are obliged to act 'in the best interests of the company'. Now, it is true that as Dine and Koutsias (2007: 189) point out, 'directors owe their duties to that legal person "the company" rather than to shareholders or potential shareholders', and directors' duties can only be enforced by the *company* suing directors. Following *Percival* v. *Wright* [1902], it has been held that directors owe their duties directly to the company and not to individual shareholders.

However, with the exception of Boatright (1994), there is little evidence to suggest that stakeholder theorists reject a view of management as agents for a principal – a role which assumes, according to Jensen and Meckling (1976: 309), 'a contract under which one or more persons (the principal(s)) engage another person (the agent) to perform some service on their behalf which involves delegating some decision making authority to the agent'. The principal–agent relationship provides a framework, consistent with a contractual view of the firm, for understanding how managers could have the authority to act on behalf of the company. It is in this context that the obligation of management to act in the best interests of the company can be understood. Managers, as agents, receive delegated authority from a principal.

The question is: who is the principal? If the principal is the company itself, then we need to ask whose interests can constitute the purpose of the company. For reasons given above, the interests pursued by the company cannot contradict the interests of those who have invested their property in it. This group logically excludes non-shareholders whose relationship with the company is one of exchange: the property they trade must be distinct from that of the company. However, the basic condition for a company's incorporation is the signing of the memorandum of association by the shareholders, who invest their property in the corporation as a means to pursue their own interests.

Therefore, although directors owe their duty to the 'company', the objectives which the company can legally pursue can be seen as coterminous with the interests of the members. This is despite the fact that shareholders lack the right to control company property and do not enter directly into acts of exchange with other stakeholders. Shareholders 'delegate' authority to management to direct the property of the corporation in pursuit of their interests (notwithstanding differences of interest between individual shareholders). Delegation of authority is *not* the same thing as a direct act of exchange, which is the relationship that other stakeholders have with the corporation.

Therefore, unlike those of other stakeholders, the ends of shareholders need not be logically separate from those of the corporation.

By this reasoning, it seems that the association of property holders whose interests are represented by the corporation can only be the shareholders. Because of the rights of property and contract that are necessary for market exchange, the objective of the corporation cannot contradict the shareholders' interests. It follows that if a corporation is understood as a legal individual with no more coercive power than a private person, then in the context of a market economy a stakeholder approach cannot be defended.

Conclusion

If a moral philosophy that applies to individuals (such as Phillips's (2003) 'Principle of Fairness') is applied to the corporation, there are certain empirical limits within which the principles can be applied. This chapter suggests that if the corporation is not seen as a public entity with the sovereign power of a state, it should instead be seen as primarily a commercial entity, in the sense supported by the legal and historical evidence given. If this market-based view of the firm is accepted, along with the context of a market economy, this also means accepting a minimal set of ethical principles that would be present in any market economy (i.e., property and contract rights). Whatever ethical principles are used to defend stakeholder theory, such as 'fairness', for example, the normative conclusion must still be consistent with property and contract rights.

If these ethical rights are applied to the empirical premises that go with a contractual and commercial view of the firm, then the *shareholder* objective appears logically as the only objective that a corporation can have. This result implies that stakeholder theory must treat the corporation, in an empirical sense, not only as a private commercial association that trades *with* stakeholders, but also as a joint association of *all* stakeholders to which some variant of the social contract theory can be applied. The coherence of this approach as a solution for stakeholder theory will now be examined.

5 | The corporation as a sovereign power in a market economy

The previous chapter argued that if the corporation is seen as a private association created to achieve its purposes through market exchange, then in the ethical framework of a market economy its objectives are reducible to the interests of shareholders alone. Therefore, the branch of stakeholder theory that relies upon principles valid for private individuals cannot produce a justified argument against the shareholder objective. However, this chapter turns to a more prominent branch of stakeholder theory and asks whether it is possible to conceive of the corporation as something *other* than a commercial entity, and if so whether this conception is compatible with the stakeholder approach in a market economy.

As shown in Chapter 3, the philosophical theories this branch of stakeholder theory draws upon suggest that the corporation has a power with respect to its stakeholders analogous to the power of a state over its subjects. If a 'social contract' (in the classical sense) exists between stakeholders, this implies that a mutuality of interests is brought together in the creation of a corporation. What is '*Bona fide* for the benefit of the company' in law would not then be reducible to the interests of the shareholders. As shown earlier, the philosophical idea of the social contract holds that a contract is formed between all members of society (not between a few to be imposed on the rest) and reflects a common interest that all have in forming a state. With respect to this common interest, all are to be considered equal under the law of the state. If the theory is used as a justification for a stakeholder approach, then such an equality of interests between stakeholders would imply that the corporation is not merely a commercial entity that trades with stakeholders, but is an association of *all* stakeholders united for a mutual purpose. The objectives of a corporation would then reflect this mutual purpose and take into account the interests of all stakeholders, rather than being concerned only with shareholder value.

This chapter calls such an understanding of the corporation into question. For a range of reasons, it is doubtful whether a business corporation can be said to possess the same qualities that are given to the state through a social contract, at least not if the traditional version of the theory is adhered to. Five main criticisms of this position are presented. The first two consider the corporation as a contractual entity engaged in market exchange. It is asked whether a mutual interest of all stakeholders can be assumed when parties to a trade have different subjective values for the objects being traded and a qualitative difference exists between stakeholders with respect to their relationship with management. The third criticism asks whether a precorporate 'State of Nature', common to all stakeholders and a necessary condition for a corporate social contract, can be said to exist. The fourth concerns the reason for the formation of the state in the social contract tradition, the purpose of *self-preservation*, and asks if it is a potential reason for all stakeholders to form a corporation. The fifth criticism considers if some of the legal processes that ensure a level of corporate accountability effectively undermine any analogy with the sovereign power of the state.

Stakeholder theory and the corporation as a commercial entity

It has been suggested that if the corporation is viewed solely as a private commercial entity it cannot accommodate any version of stakeholder theory. It can now be argued that stakeholder theory is incompatible with a commercial view of the corporation in any sense at all. The two principal reasons are as follows.

First, if the corporation has any goals which it cannot achieve without market exchange, and (with the possible exception of local communities, shareholders and the government) this exchange is with stakeholders,[1] then it is logically impossible for it to pursue the interests of all these groups simultaneously. A necessary condition for trade is that the goods being exchanged are valued differently by the parties to the trade. If this condition is not fulfilled and both parties place

---

[1] Employees, financiers and customers are all considered specific stakeholder groups for Freeman (1994: 417), and Sacconi (2004: 7) considers a stakeholder in a 'strict sense' to be one 'locked in' by his or her specific investment, which includes all those groups with which a business conducts commercial transactions.

an identical subjective value on the same good, then whatever one is prepared to offer the other in exchange (in order to improve its own situation) would leave the other worse off. It follows that when a corporation as a legal individual trades with stakeholders, it places a different value on the good being exchanged (e.g., labour time) than is placed on it by the other party (e.g., an employee). If a worker values one hour of his or her labour time at £5 and the company he or she works for also values it at £5, then everything else being equal, there will be no incentive to trade.

It follows that if each person is attempting through an exchange to achieve precisely the same end, and each person is assumed to be equally rational (so that there are no differences in their evaluation of the best means to the end), then their subjective valuations of a set of goods as a means to the end will not differ, and this takes away the incentive to trade. Therefore it can be argued, insofar as the corporation trades with stakeholders to achieve its ends, that these ends must be distinct from the purposes of its stakeholders. It follows that the interests the corporate objective can represent must be distinguishable from the interests of non-shareholding stakeholders, and there can be no unanimity of interests expressed in a contract of every stakeholder with every other. The corporation as a commercial entity therefore cannot be understood as a 'social contract'.[2]

It can be asked how it is logically impossible for managers to pursue the interests of all stakeholders when, as Freeman et al. (2010) plausibly argue, managers cannot create value sustainably for any one stakeholder if they routinely ignore the interests of the rest. As I argued in Chapter 1, a distinction needs to be made between the necessity of paying attention to value creation through trade with stakeholders, and the pursuit of a purpose that is ultimately reducible to the interests of all stakeholders. Recognition of this difference is in fact apparent in Freeman et al.'s comment: 'We prefer the metaphor of thinking about keeping stakeholder interests in "harmony". "Harmony" depicts a "jointness" to the interests... *The notes are different* but they must blend together' (2010: 27, emphasis added).

---

[2] Although the focus here is on corporations, the argument applies equally to noncorporate business owners and partnerships. The basic point remains that the property and immediate ends of stakeholders who trade with a business cannot be identical to the property and ends of the business itself.

An analogy from academia will illustrate the point. A successful university lecturer has to satisfy jointly the interests of many academic stakeholders: students, funding bodies, heads of department, co-authors, journal editors, etc. However, it is not inconsistent to say that an academic cannot represent, as an end, the ends of all these stakeholders.[3] For example, students write essays so that they can get good grades and graduate with prospects of a good career. However, sometimes we have to fail students to uphold academic standards. In 2006, lecturers in the United Kingdom went on strike and refused to mark students' exams, preventing their graduation, in order to improve academic salaries. The fact that the aims of lecturers are not identical to the aims of other academic stakeholders is clearly a reality of academic life. In the field of business, the 'social contract' model assumes that the aims of stakeholders *can* be reduced to one common aim pursued by corporate managers.

Second, there is a crucial difference between the relationship a corporation has with its stakeholders and the relationship between a sovereign and its subjects in the social contract tradition. Despite the earlier point about the inconsistent interests of stakeholders in a commercial view of the corporation, there has been a tendency among stakeholder theorists to view the corporation as a voluntary contract of all stakeholders united for a common purpose. Freeman (1994: 415) describes the corporation as 'a contractual process among those parties affected' and Sacconi (2006: 266) sees it as a 'coalition' of stakeholders engaged in a joint productive activity.[4] McNulty (1975: 579) claims that managerial authority must be democratic rather than autocratic

---

[3] When an applicant for an academic position is asked: 'Where do you see yourself in 5 years' time?' it is not generally expected that they will answer: 'this depends on where students, co-authors, journal editors, reviewers and funding bodies would like me to be' – though neither is it doubted that to be successful they will need to pay attention to the interests of most of these groups.

[4] Both drawing heavily on Rawls, it is possible that Freeman (1994) and Sacconi (2006) take advantage of an ambiguity in Rawls's (1999: 4) definition of 'society': 'a cooperative venture for mutual advantage'. Rawls's definition could be held to cover a business corporation but seems to lack those features that would make it equivalent to a state. However, it would need to be a state if (by the traditional theory of the social contract) it could legitimately distribute wealth and use a monopoly on coercion to protect basic liberties. This makes it possible for stakeholder theorists to treat the corporation as a 'society' in the Rawlsian sense and give it statelike powers over its stakeholders – a move which is conceptually problematic but consistent with Rawls's own definitions.

because employees have a Lockean 'right to property found in the application of human expertise, the human factor of production'. Just as Locke claimed that any government not based on consent would violate the natural rights of the community, organisational goals are not the exclusive property of management but are 'subject to some sort of accountability to all employees, those who possess rights derived from human input ... As such, management becomes an elite whose authority rests on the consent of the governed' (1975: 579–80). The analogy with the state is here quite explicit: a corporation is not just a voluntary union of stakeholder interests, but has the right (through management) to 'govern' them within the limits of their consent, as expressed through democratic participation.

In exploring whether an analogy with the state can be used to describe the powers that management is authorised to exercise by stakeholders, Hobbes's (1651/1996: 106–10) ideas on 'persons' and 'authors' are instructive. Hobbes writes that a person whose words 'are considered as his own is called a *natural person*: and when they are considered as representing the words and actions of another, then he is a feigned or *artificial person*' (1651/1996: 106, emphases in original). Hobbes points out that the Latin word *persona* signifies 'the *disguise*, or *outward appearance* of a man, counterfeited on the stage ... and from the stage, hath been translated to any representer of speech and action, as well in tribunals, as theatres' (ibid., emphases in original). Therefore, 'a *person*, is the same that an *actor* is ... and to *personate*, is to *act*, or *represent* himself, or another' (1651/1996: 106–7). After this overview of the connection between a 'person' or 'actor' and representation, Hobbes discusses what it means to *authorise* an actor. He writes that the words and actions of an artificial person are *owned* by those whom they represent: 'the person is the *actor*; and he that owneth his words and actions, is the AUTHOR: in which case the actor acteth by authority ... So that by authority, is always understood a right of doing any act: and *done by authority*, done by commission, or license from him whose right it is' (1651/1996: 107, emphases in original).[5]

---

[5] For Hobbes, the exceptions are persons who represent inanimate objects (such as when a rector or overseer represents a hospital or church), irrational people (such as when guardians personate children), an idol (e.g., heathen gods personated by officers of the state) and even the true God (who was personated by Moses) (1651/1996: 108).

Following the brief discussion of the legal nature of the corporation in the previous chapter, the relationship between shareholders
and managers could be seen in terms of an author and actor. It can
be said that the means by which shareholders authorise management
is the memorandum of association (in UK law), which specifies the
basic purpose of the company.[6] Hobbes writes: 'no man is obliged
by a covenant, whereof he is not the author; nor consequently by a
covenant made against, or beside the authority' (1651/1996: 107), and
shareholders indeed are not considered legally or morally culpable for
actions taken by management outside the scope of what a company is
able legally to do.

However, one cannot say that the other stakeholders of a corporation *authorise* management to act on their behalf. If the fact that
a corporation trades with a given stakeholder implies a divergence in
their immediate interests, then a unanimous decision by *all* stakeholders to authorise management to act in their joint interest cannot be
assumed. In an evaluation of the social contract method in business,
Keeley (1995: 248) writes: 'participants need not agree on common
goals or ends, but may treat organizations as means to their separate
ends.' He continues:

Organizations exist to achieve some common good or objective, and it seems
logical to evaluate organizations on the basis of whether they attain their
goals. The trouble is that organizational participants rarely agree on what
these common goods or goals are . . . People participate in organizations for
all sorts of reasons: shareholders for profits, workers for wages, customers
for services, etc. And which of these outcomes are considered *organizational*
goals seems to depend on whose viewpoint one adopts. (1995: 250, emphasis
in original)

If this characterisation of the relationships between stakeholders and
the firm is correct, then the corporation as a legal 'person' cannot
'personate' (i.e., *represent*) the interests of all stakeholders at any
one time. An association of stakeholder interests realised through the

---

[6] However, the purpose of the company was removed from the memorandum
when the 2006 Companies Act in the United Kingdom came into force in 2009.
The articles of association will be left to specify any limits on what the company
may do, though it is up to shareholders to enforce this internally, and it cannot
be imposed on the company from outside (Dine and Koutsias 2007: 46).

corporation as a 'social contract' is by this reasoning thrown into doubt.

This argument also raises questions for Scherer and Palazzo's (2007, 2011) 'political' conception of CSR. As described in Chapter 2, they argue that corporations have a democratic responsibility to provide public goods and regulation where states are unable to do so. This responsibility is both made legitimate and discharged through a proactive engagement with civil society. However, if management is assumed to be an agent acting on behalf of some principal, then the relevant question here is: who *authorises* corporate management to act? In other words, who *entrusts* managers with the resources to carry out their specific duties, and to whom are they ultimately accountable? If the answer to these questions is simply the 'demos' or 'the people', then we need to ask how 'the people' come to authorise management to act on their behalf. It is uncontroversial to say that there are corporate activities aimed at 'doing good' for society that could benefit from the involvement of a wide range of affected parties and experts. But it is quite another thing to claim that directors are actually accountable to the 'demos' for the results of such activities.[7] Especially in the case of 'failed states', there is here an additional need to show how the relevant 'demos' is identified.[8]

By comparison, Hobbes's theory of persons and authors provides an account of how the sovereign is authorised by the people. Hobbes (1651/1996: 109) points out that as 'the multitude naturally is not *one*, but *many*', unity cannot be understood in multitude other than by being represented by one person: 'it is the *unity* of the representer, not the *unity* of the represented, that maketh the person *one*' (ibid.). It follows that although a multitude may be made a unity through one representative, each member of the multitude remains separately an author of all that the person does in his or her name: 'they cannot be understood for one; but for many authors, of every thing their representative saith, or doth in their name; every man giving their common representer, authority from himself in particular; and owning

---

[7] Cf. Höpfl's (2008) perceptive analysis of the idea of 'democratic accountability' in the context of business and public administration.

[8] As explained in Chapter 2, a full analysis of Scherer and Palazzo's position is beyond the scope of the present discussion, but it should not affect the logic of the argument here.

all the actions the representer doth' (ibid.). For Hobbes the state arises in this manner. The only way in which men may erect a common power to keep them all in awe is 'to confer all their power and strength upon one man, or assembly of men, that may reduce all their wills, by plurality of voices, unto one will' (1651/1996: 114). In this, everyone acknowledges himself 'to be author of whatsoever he that so beareth their person, shall act, or cause to be acted' (ibid.). He who carries this person is called the *sovereign*, and subjects are 'bound, every man to every man, to own, and be reputed author of all, that he that already is sovereign, shall do, and judge fit to be done' (1651/1996: 115).

A crucial difference between the authorisation that for Hobbes gives rise to the state, and that which underpins the accountability of managers to shareholders, is the existence of *accountability* in the latter relation. As Skinner (1989: 15) points out, Hobbes and other writers in the sixteenth and seventeenth centuries (such as Suarez and Bodin) who challenge the idea that the powers of government merely reflect the powers of the people admit that political power is originally instituted by the people, but argue that an 'absolute transfer' takes place from the people to the sovereign. This means that unlike the shareholder–manager relation, the people of a state do not 'delegate' their authority to the sovereign, but altogether alienate it. As will be argued later, the lack of accountability of the sovereign power is a sharp difference between a sovereign state on the one hand and a business corporation on the other.

It could be argued that in another branch of social contract theory (that to which Locke and Rousseau belong) the rulers of the state are accountable to the body of the people just as a board of directors is accountable to a body of shareholders (or in theory, stakeholders). For these authors, sovereign authority is *not* alienated by the people. Contrary to Hobbes, the power of government is restricted by the will of the people in which sovereignty resides. Rousseau calls this the 'General Will' and Locke calls it the 'Community' or 'the People'. Rousseau (1762/1968: 70) expresses the inalienable nature of sovereign power when he writes that for the acts of the sovereign to constitute law, they must be the will of the whole body of the people (expressed through majority vote), and that each individual has an equal share in the sovereign authority (1762/1968: 103). Rousseau goes on to state clearly: 'Sovereignty cannot be represented, for the same reason that it cannot be alienated; its essence is the general will, and will cannot be represented' (1762/1968: 141). A similar position is taken by Locke, who argues that all legislative power (and by implication executive power) can be overthrown if the people judge that the 'unalterable Law of *Self-Preservation*, for which they entered into Society' has been invaded (1689/1988: 367, emphasis in original). Locke writes that the 'Supream Power' never leaves 'the People', so it can remove the legislative if it acts contrary to the trust reposed in it (ibid.).

However, whether sovereignty is 'alienated' or not, what is crucial in a comparison with the business corporation is that sovereign power is held to receive its authority from the united will of all the people. It is a voluntary union arising through a rational judgement of how to realise a joint interest (i.e., self-preservation) through the state. This is why Rousseau writes of finding a form of association 'under which each individual, while uniting himself with the others, obeys no one but himself, and remains as free as before' (1762/1968: 60) and that subjects who submit to the social contract 'obey nobody but their own will' (1762/1968: 77). For Kant also: 'The legislative authority can belong only to the united will of the people. For since all right is to proceed from it, it *cannot* do anyone wrong by its law' (1797/1996: 91, emphasis in original). And for Hobbes (1651: 114) the covenant of society is of 'every man with every man', and the multitude so united (a 'Commonwealth') is 'one person, of whose acts a great multitude, by mutual covenants one with another, have made themselves every one, the author' (ibid.).

However, it is difficult to see the business corporation (with management as its executive) arising through the united will of all the stakeholders. If the corporation is viewed as a commercial entity that trades with its stakeholders in a competitive market, then there cannot be the homogeneity of purpose necessary for all stakeholders as a body to constitute the corporation and authorise its actions in their name. States of course also trade with some citizens (e.g., public sector employees and suppliers), but this fact is assumed to be independent of the sovereign's moral authority to govern. There are citizens with whom states do not trade and noncitizens with whom they do: the 'social contract' on which the legitimacy of the state depends is not in theory contingent upon commercial relationships.

It is worth noting Rousseau's belief that even under the social contract there is a divergence between the private will of individuals and the general will (1762/1968: 69). However, he asserts not only that if the deviations are small and no 'sectional associations' are allowed to form then the differences will cancel out and the general will prevails (1762/1968: 72–3), but also that it is an initial *harmony* of interests that makes the establishment of civil society possible (1762/1968: 69). The concept of a business corporation bargaining with its stakeholders in a competitive market does not seem to suggest such unanimity of interests. In fact, in speaking of Rawls's theory and the possibility of its application to business, Keeley writes:

> Rawlsian primary goods still presuppose too much homogeneity of purpose to allow for the variability of ends that participants pursue in individual corporations (say, in corporations, where some shareholders seek profits but not necessarily power, workers seek wages or security or self-fulfilment in varying degrees, customers seek goods or services but not occupational opportunity, and so forth). The problem is that different organizations serve different instrumental functions for different participants, even though all the organizations that constitute society or a person's sphere of action may serve a common instrumental function taken as a whole. (1995: 250)

It seems therefore that it is not possible to view the corporation as simultaneously embodying a social contract and a commercial purpose. However, given the argument that the corporation considered simply as a commercial entity seems compatible only with the shareholder view, it is necessary to ask whether it can be seen as a statelike entity with sovereign power, leaving aside its commercial purposes. It is interesting to note McMahon's (1995: 302) observation that *if* one accepts an 'agency model' of the corporation, 'all employees have the moral status of agents of the corporate principal'. According to this model: 'the corporate principal is a legal instrument . . . that enables the shareholders to achieve their purposes. Thus for managers to serve as agents of the corporate principal is ultimately for them to serve as trustees for the shareholders. If the model of agency is correct, then, managers should adopt the standpoint of the shareholders when determining organizational policy' (ibid.).

However, McMahon argues that managerial authority does not have to be seen this way. It can be seen as 'cooperation-facilitating authority', which implies that managers function as trustees for the employees:

> Legally, the employees of an organization are its agents, but for normative theory, the organization is like a *state*, an entity created by the acceptance

by its members of a mutually beneficial cooperative scheme. Authority of this sort can be democratically exercised, in which case the people from whose standpoint the moral questions confronting the organization are to be decided (the employees) will make these decisions collectively, or elect people to make them. (1995: 303, emphasis added)

Here McMahon makes clear that the only alternative to seeing managers as agents for shareholders (as supported by a market-based view of the corporation) is instead to see the corporation as 'like a state' or a 'mutually beneficial cooperative scheme' (in the Rawlsian language he uses).

To see the corporation as something other than a private association formed through market contracts is not necessarily to see it as incompatible with a market economy. One of the principles of a market economy defended earlier was a basic right of contract (with the corresponding duties and claim-rights of performing and expecting performance of a contract), and it is not contrary to this right for stakeholders to establish an association with powers to achieve a common purpose. A common point in social contract theory is that the 'contract' is voluntarily entered, so there is no *prima facie* inconsistency between seeing the corporation as a contract of this sort and the basic rights of a market economy. Therefore, the next section asks whether there is evidence for the existence of such a contract in the formation of the corporation.

Stakeholder theory and the corporation as a 'social contract'

To envisage the corporation as possessing the same qualities as a state legitimately established through a 'social contract' it is necessary to consider *why* individuals might consent to establish a corporation in this form. If one examines the existing written contracts that constitute the legal obligations of any corporation, it is unlikely one will find the express consent of all 'stakeholders' (actual/potential employees, customers, suppliers, the local community, management, etc.) authorising the corporation to regulate their conduct through the coercive power of law and to act as the final judge in resolving disputes between them.[9] Assuming that no express consent can be found in the

---

[9] This is not to say that corporations historically have never performed such roles. Williston (1888) writes of how the earliest business corporations in the

case of any given corporation, what must be assumed instead is tacit consent. The previous chapter touched upon the difficulty of identifying consent. However, what is important is not whether consent can be identified – this assumption can be granted if a social contract is said to exist – but rather the methodological problem of establishing *what* is being consented to. In social contract theory this problem is solved by positing a 'State of Nature' which any rational person would wish to avoid. As a result of this rationality, a person who enjoys security in the territory of a sovereign state is assumed to give tacit consent to the sovereign power. The problem is whether a precorporate 'State of Nature' can be assumed for the stakeholders of a business corporation.

The best-known attempt to defend specific social responsibilities for business through the device of a hypothetical 'State of Nature', the disadvantages of which are solved by allowing the formation of productive organisations, is that of Thomas Donaldson (1982: 36–57) in *Corporations and Morality*. Donaldson (1982: 42) writes that parties to his contract are society and business, where 'business' refers to all productive organisations (not limited to corporations) and 'society' refers to all individual members of society (rather than some 'supra-individual social entity'). In considering the question of what society stands to gain from allowing productive organisations to form, he writes: 'it is not obvious precisely why societies should allow them to exist, that is, what specific benefits society should hope to gain from the bargain' (1982: 43). He claims: 'Only one assumption can be made readily: that the members of society should demand at a minimum that the benefits from authorising the existence of productive organizations outweigh the detriments of doing so' (1982: 44). He then recommends a return to a device in social contract theory of imagining what society would be like without the institution being analysed.

He proceeds to set out a list of advantages that consumers (understood as all who invest in a corporation) and workers stand to gain

fifteenth and sixteenth centuries (preceded by the guilds) had the function of regulating a particular branch of trade, and the municipal peace guilds of medieval times (a form of 'civil corporation') had responsibility for the security of their members. The British East India Company of course had its own army. The question, however, is whether the groups considered to be the stakeholders of a modern business corporation have a joint reason for establishing a corporation with *all* the powers of the sovereign state.

from the existence of productive organisations, and a list of disadvantages they would seek to avoid. Amongst the former are improving efficiency for consumers, stabilising levels of output and channels of distribution, increasing the income potential for employees and their capacity for social contributions and diffusing personal liability (1982: 45–9). Some of the drawbacks include pollution and the depletion of natural resources, the misuse of political power, worker alienation, monotony and the dehumanisation of the worker (1982: 49–52). Donaldson argues that from the standpoint of the social contract between productive organisations and society, the benefits to the worker and consumer 'constitute a set of reasons which rational people living in a state of individual production might use to justify the introduction of productive organizations' (1982: 49), but these organisations would be obliged to minimise the drawbacks, and hence *'enhance the welfare of society through a satisfaction of consumer and worker interests'* (ibid., emphasis in original).

The important thing to observe about Donaldson's (1982) contractual justification of the corporation is that his contract exists between 'society' on the one hand and all 'productive organisations', considered independently from society, on the other.[10] What is not proposed is a contract of each potential stakeholder with every other in forming a single corporation. Whatever the merits[11] of Donaldson's hypothetical 'state of individual production' and resulting contract between productive organisations and society, it does not explain how an individual corporation might acquire purposes in relation to its stakeholders' interests. Besides, once the very first business corporation is formed, Donaldson's 'state of individual production' no longer exists and the

[10]   The separateness of the two parties is implied by the fact that there is a contract *between* them. If productive organisations were considered part of society, this would amount to society forming a contract with part of itself, which is not possible if a contract is the union of two separate wills (Kant 1797/1996).

[11]   Hodapp (1990: 128) argues persuasively that Donaldson's '"social contract" is not that, rather it is an account of the benefits that society reasonably may expect to receive from corporations as productive organizations'. It follows that 'Donaldson's social contract theory as a methodology is circular, presupposing the information which it is supposed to generate. That is, one already builds in the purposes of an institution before engaging in the imaginative experiment' (ibid.). This criticism receives support from Conry (1995: 202): 'It is at least arguable that Donaldson's conclusions do not follow from the analysis of the pre-organization state of nature; they follow instead from his correct *intuitions*' (emphasis in original).

reasons that any group of stakeholders might subsequently form a corporation cannot be derived from the 'State of Nature' argument that Donaldson (1982) offers.

Indeed, this point can be illustrated with Donaldson's later writings. In *Ties That Bind: A Social Contracts Approach to Business Ethics*, Donaldson and Dunfee (1999: 19) distinguish between 'macro' contracts which are 'broad, hypothetical agreements among rational people . . . designed to establish objective background standards for social interaction' and 'micro' contracts which are 'extant' and reflect an actual agreement within a community (ibid.). They link the former kind to the traditional social contract theories of Locke and Rawls (which form the basis of Donaldson's (1982) contract between productive organisations and society) and the latter to 'agreements existing within and among industries, national economic systems, *corporations*, trade associations, and so on' (ibid., emphasis added). This implies that for Donaldson and Dunfee (1999), the sort of 'contract' which is relevant within an actual corporation is a 'micro' contract of 'extant' agreements. The authors argue that in identifying stakeholder obligations for a given organisation, 'one looks more closely to identify relevant community norms indicating how the line should be drawn between shareholder and stakeholder interests. Under a contractarian approach the question is transformed into an empirical one of identifying dominant legitimate norms' (1999: 251).

Whilst an explanation of Donaldson and Dunfee's (1999) position in the context of their full argument (which they call *Integrative Social Contracts Theory* (ISCT)) is unnecessary here, it is sufficient to note that they consider the contractual obligations of a corporation to its stakeholders to be determined not in the first place by a tacit 'macro' contract between all members of society, but by the express 'micro' agreements actually reached between a corporation and its various stakeholders. If one looks at the written contracts drawn up between any corporation and its stakeholders, including the memorandum and articles of association approved by the shareholders, one will not find a document signed by every supplier, customer, employee, manager, etc., to establish a corporation with sovereign powers of physical coercion and judicial authority. To my knowledge, no 'express' consent or 'micro' contract of this kind exists for any business corporation.

Heugens et al. (2006: 214), in discussing how a contractual scheme for the corporation can be characterised, argue that 'the distinction between real and hypothetical consent is largely irrelevant to our understanding of what constitutes a contractual scheme and what not'. While a contractual scheme *might* rely on the existence of 'real' or 'express' consent, 'which can be traced back to a founding document or explicit contractual promise' (ibid.), or 'hypothetical' consent underpinning a 'macro' contract, what Donaldson and Dunfee (1999) argue is that an individual corporation cannot be understood in terms of the latter, but only in terms of express agreements. This does not point to an association of all stakeholders analogous to a 'macro' social contract encompassing every member of society.

It might be asked why a business corporation cannot be seen in terms of a 'macro' contract. Is this because there is no 'State of Nature' equally afflicting all stakeholders prior to a particular corporation being formed, and to which all would see a particular corporation as the solution? An obvious response would be that with regard to the stakeholders of a corporation prior to its formation, nothing can be said of the interests they desire to fulfil through transacting with that corporation without empirical knowledge of their needs and wants. This in turn is entirely contingent upon their ability to satisfy these desires through existing economic arrangements, and any theory requiring contingent empirical knowledge cannot use hypothetical premises to generate any more than a hypothetical conclusion. Also, the very fact that stakeholders can be divided into separate groups – customers, employees, suppliers, etc. – or different subcategories within these groups (Friedman and Miles 2006: 14) is evidence of the variety of ways in which stakeholders seek to satisfy their needs through a corporation. An assumption necessary for the hypothetical 'State of Nature' to generate the same conclusions for all contractors is that all have the same preferences and are equally rational (i.e., all choose the same equally efficient means to a given end), which runs contrary to the fact that stakeholders seek to satisfy their needs in *different* ways relative to the corporation. This again implies there is no initial situation in which all stakeholders are *equal* prior to establishing a corporation.

Although not mentioning corporations specifically, this argument is consistent with the following observation of Heugens et al. (2006: 220):

In contrast to the macro-social contract, which is typically portrayed as a universally compelling conclusion concerning rights and obligations that every rational contractor ought to obey, the overlap between the contractors' motivations to enter a microsocial contract is seldom perfect... Here, all parties to the contract see a reason for cooperation, but the nature of these reasons differs from contractor to contractor. Examples include learning alliances, supply agreements, professional partnerships, membership organizations, and joint ventures. (2006: 220)

A similar point is made by Phillips (2003: 50), who discusses the role of *meritocracy* in organisations and contrasts this with the state, in which 'no relevantly similar person should be treated differently by the state *qua citizen*. Civil society is not a meritocracy' (emphasis in original). He writes that an organisation's stakeholders are not 'radically equal' in the way that citizens in the 'original position' (Rawls's version of the 'State of Nature') are assumed to be. While Phillips would not presumably wish to deny that an organisation's stakeholders are *morally* equal, he writes: 'Some contribute more to an organization's specific goals and thus have "legitimate expectations" (to use Rawls's terminology) to a greater portion of the benefits of organizational efforts. This inequality renders an organizational original position argument exponentially more complex' (2003: 50–1). What he highlights is that stakeholders make different levels of contribution to an organisation and (by his 'principle of fairness') are entitled to different levels of benefit.

What this implies is that not all stakeholders are expected to benefit in the same way from the organisation. This would be the case, however, if there was a universal 'State of Nature' which gave all an equal interest in forming a corporation. If we return to 'traditional' social contract theory, the passage cited from Phillips (2003: 50–1) can be compared with the following passage on taxation in Hobbes's *Leviathan*:

To equal justice, appertaineth also the equal imposition of taxes; the equality whereof dependeth not on the equality of riches, but on the equality of the debt, that every man oweth to the commonwealth for his defence... For the impositions, that are laid on the people by the sovereign power, are nothing else but the wages, due to them that hold the public sword, to defend private men in the exercise of their several trades, and callings. Seeing then the benefit that every one receiveth thereby, is the enjoyment of life, which is equally dear to poor, and rich; the debt which a poor man oweth them that defend his life, is the same which a rich man oweth for the defence of his...the equality of imposition, consisteth rather in the equality of that which is consumed, than of the riches of the persons that consume the same. (1651/1996: 229)

This passage clearly illustrates the equal interest that all members of society are held to have in the existence of a sovereign power (who holds the 'public sword'), and consequently the equal contribution and benefit expected of each. It is of course possible for Hobbes to make this claim because of the equality that his 'State of Nature' gives to every individual upon entering society. The fact that the stakeholders of a corporation make very different levels of contribution and are rewarded in very different ways (compare the contributions made by an occasional customer and an employee winning a long-term service award) implies that they cannot be considered to have an *equal* interest in the existence of the same corporation. Still less can it be assumed that the stakeholders of *any* corporation necessarily have an equal interest in its existence.

The conclusion must be that a 'State of Nature' common to all stakeholders of a corporation cannot be said to exist. This implies that a corporation cannot represent in its objectives a joint interest of all stakeholders collectively, which was a vital condition of this branch of stakeholder theory. However, rather than asking whether a 'State of Nature' can be imagined for all stakeholders of a corporation, it can instead be asked whether the purpose of the *state* envisioned in social contract theory is a purpose that all stakeholders could share in establishing a corporation. If the arguments to this point are correct then the answer should be that there is no equivalent purpose, yet it is worth examining as a question in its own right. If the conclusion remains that no common stakeholder interest can be found to constitute the corporate objective, then it must be concluded that the social contract theory as applied to corporations *cannot* yield a normative stakeholder theory.

Phillips (2003) argues that if contributions and benefits with respect to an organisation differ between stakeholders, and organisations can be seen as *meritocracies*, then another difference between states and (non-state) organisations is that unlike states, other types of organisation can have specific goals and aims. It follows for Phillips that in addition to all the complexities with which Rawls's own theory is faced, any application of his 'original position' to an organisation must stipulate the goal of the group and what is to count as contributing to that goal, as well as who is to be included in the 'original position deliberations' and what psychological attributes they have (2003: 51). Phillips argues that states (and 'societies') are rather different from private organisations, thereby throwing doubt on the applicability of social contract theory to organisations: 'There are no ends of a well-ordered society in the way that there are for other associations . . . the state should be neutral in its preference for any particular set of values, other than those that permit individual liberty in choosing a conception of the good and living by it' (2003: 48–9).

Moriarty (2005) takes up this point (focusing on a previous paper by Phillips and Margolis, 1999) and argues to the contrary that it does at least have the *implication* of some specific goal that a society, even a 'neutralist liberal state', might pursue:

For the assumption that neutralist liberal states have no goals, and hence no place for contribution-assessment, is false. Although their goals may be different than those of other states, neutralist liberal states do have goals. One of these, of course, is to remain neutral among different conceptions of the good. Thus, as Phillips and Margolis themselves recognise, the neutralist liberal state will have as a goal ensuring that its citizens have the liberty to pursue their conceptions of the good. But this liberty can be meaningfully exercised only when certain material conditions of life obtain, and this demands the pursuit of other more specific goals. The neutralist liberal state will therefore also have as a goal protecting its citizens' lives and property. (2005: 458)

The argument that even a state that is neutral between individual conceptions of the good still has an overall goal of maintaining peace and security and protecting life and property resonates with the various social contract philosophies examined earlier. For Hobbes, Locke, Rousseau, Kant and to an extent Rawls also, the central motivation for forming society is security and self-preservation. It follows that an essential objective of the sovereign power must be the preservation of order, stability and the security of the lives and property of the subjects over which it is authorised to rule. The applicability of this objective to the business corporation should now be examined.

The main concern with a corporate objective such as this is that a business corporation is already a *legal* artefact. It is constituted in law as a *legal* individual. If the corporation is indeed a contract of all its stakeholders, then the decision to establish a corporation would presuppose the existence of a legal system to which these stakeholders are already subject. The corporation could not be established as a sovereign power in its own right, as one would already have to exist in order for it to come into being. Therefore, one cannot move from a desire for self-preservation to the creation of a sovereign power (with a monopoly on the means of violence) as the best means for ensuring this, if such a power is already in place. The move is illogical and cannot be a rational solution for the stakeholders of a business corporation.

That corporations cannot be considered as existing (normatively or empirically) outside the context of legal and political institutions is acknowledged in many texts of stakeholder theory.[12] Phillips (2003: 44–5) writes:

The ethics of associations and civil society within a Rawlsian framework assume a just basic structure. So applying to organizations the mechanisms and principles used to create a just basic structure is tantamount to designing traffic laws in accord with the laws of human flight . . . How organizations are to be arranged depends upon the way the basic structure is arranged.

Phillips goes on to say that unlike private organisations, 'the basic structure institutions are generally considered to have a monopoly on the legitimate use of force. Basic structure institutions may physically compel compliance with its mandates in a way that private organizations may not' (2003: 47). This supports the point that corporations cannot be seen as independent of the legally coercive institutions under whose jurisdiction they exist. Cragg (2002: 128), while arguing against the shareholder model of the firm, writes 'corporations are not simply artifacts; they are *legal* artifacts . . . a legal framework of a particular character is a necessary condition for the existence of corporations' – an implication of which is that 'corporations can only operate successfully within communities with functioning legal systems. Any action tending to undermine a legal system within which a corporation is nested is a potential threat to the corporation itself' (ibid.).

---

[12] This is not to suggest that many of the activities of corporations (especially multinationals) do not take place in a geographical context of ineffective political institutions or weak state regulation (Crane et al. 2008; Scherer and Palazzo 2011).

Donaldson and Dunfee (1999), also defenders of the stakeholder view, write of the corporation as depending upon a legal framework for its existence: 'The social and legal institution that possesses the most profound significance for business is that of private property. Without the institution of property and its accompanying concepts and legal procedures, "business" as such would not exist' (1999: 15). Even in the case of the earliest business corporations in the sixteenth and seventeenth century, which often had a regulatory role over the trade their members were engaged in, the act of incorporation to create a company was considered very different from a 'social contract' to establish sovereign jurisdiction. Thomas Hobbes writes of the motivation for forming a corporation in his time:

> We are to consider the end, for which all men that are merchants, and may buy and sell, export, and import their merchandise, according to their own discretions, do nevertheless bind themselves up in one corporation...But this is *no body politic*, there being no common representative to oblige them to any other law, than that which is common to all other subjects. The end of their incorporating, is to make their gain the greater. (1651/1996: 153–4, emphasis added)

An assumption common to each of these authors is that the corporation exists within a legal framework which itself presumes a monopoly on the means of physical coercion to which the corporation is subject. The interest which all participants in the classical social contract were held to have equally was that of self-preservation, which led to the need for a sovereign power with a legitimate monopoly on violence and with the means to enforce order. This cannot therefore be an interest common to all stakeholders in forming a corporation.

Crane et al. (2008: 73) add the important point that voluntary corporate codes should not be seen as a legitimate substitute for the law of the state. They write:

> The crucial deficit with codes...is that in many cases they are developed without substantial input from those citizens whose rights they are supposed to be protecting and governing. In the democratic governmental realm, often constitutions emerge from, and are amended by, a democratic, or at least representative, process.

To the extent that corporations have a legislative process, it can be seen to operate rather differently to the democratic legislatures of most states. Crane et al. (2008) go on to say of corporate codes: 'As voluntary commitments, the correspondence of such initiatives with 'laws' remains rather loose, especially given that most initiatives do not impose penalties for non-compliance' (ibid.).

If we revert to viewing the corporation in terms of the market-based contracts it forms with its stakeholders, the legal context in which it operates plays an obvious role in ensuring accountability of managers to shareholders (usually through AGMs and the various corporate governance requirements placed on a corporation) and the compliance of the corporation with contracts it enters with workers, suppliers, local councils, and vice versa. In developed nations the law generally allows scope for trade union representation for workers and collective bargaining (e.g., through the National Labour Relations Act (1935) in the United States and the Trade Union and Labour Relations Act (1992) in the United Kingdom). The details of such arrangements are not of concern here. Rather, the very existence of such arrangements of accountability and bargaining illustrates another fundamental difference between a sovereign state in a 'social contract' with its members, and a corporation in relation to its stakeholders. In short, 'the people' of a state cannot hold to account the sovereign power or bargain with it because either they *are* the sovereign power, or they have *alienated* sovereignty to a person or assembly of people that carries the sovereign power. Either way, by what is referred to as the 'logic of sovereignty', the sovereign cannot be held accountable to anyone, as there is no higher power to judge a dispute between it and another party.

This is clear in Rousseau's (1762/1968: 135) claim that the sovereign is not bound by any previous laws and cannot form contractual obligations, one of the reasons for which is that the contracting parties would be 'without any guarantee of their reciprocal commitments' (1762/1968: 144). With no higher source of authority than the sovereign power, the sovereign itself cannot have obligations enforced upon it. Kant (1793/1991: 75) argues that each member of the commonwealth has rights of coercion in relation to all the others, except for the head of state: 'for if he too could be coerced, he would not be the head of state, and the hierarchy of subordination would ascend indefinitely'. For this reason he argues that a sovereign has rights against his subjects, but *no duties*, and 'subjects may indeed oppose . . . injustice by *complaints* but not by resistance' (1797/1996: 95). Hobbes (1651/1996: 115) is also clear that subjects have no right to change the form of government and the sovereign is *not* bound by any conditions of the contract by which the state was instituted (1651/1996: 116–17).

The idea that stakeholders might voluntarily set up a corporation that is completely unaccountable to anybody is far from plausible and highlights further the tenuousness of any link between social contract theory and corporate social responsibility. Certainly, any notion of the corporation as a commercial entity in which contractual compliance is an essential aspect of business renders an analogy with a sovereign power utterly groundless.

Conclusion

This chapter must conclude that any application of the social contract method to a business corporation is beset with problems. These concern the importance of accountability and the lack of unanimity between stakeholder interests. Both can be seen as basic to the concept of the corporation itself. However, their opposites must hold for any entity encompassing a 'social contract'. Martin Parker (2002) is perhaps right to observe, in a discussion about the idea of 'citizenship' and 'the corporate state', that 'A state, or organization, can be viewed metaphorically or discursively as a form of social contract and, if the metaphor is widespread enough, that will shape expectations and conduct' (2002: 58). However, this is not a justifiable basis for stakeholder theory.

It might be asked why so much emphasis should be placed on this tradition of political theory, when so many other approaches might be used to defend a corporate objective that includes the interests of stakeholders. Answering this question involves highlighting stakeholder theory's basic premise that the corporate objective must be compatible with the framework of a market economy. The importance of contract, property and consent as moral principles which any society recognising the legitimacy of market exchange would acknowledge (assuming moral consistency) has been identified. It follows that whatever corporate objective a stakeholder theorist defends must be consistent with the assumed consent of all property holders who invest in the corporation. If the corporation is perceived entirely as a commercial entity, then given the ethical principles of a market economy, only the interests of shareholders can coincide with those pursued by the corporation. To encompass a wider range of interests in the corporate objective, one would have to view the corporation not as a commercial entity which trades with its stakeholders but as an association of *all* its stakeholders. This is indeed the implication of the idea of a 'social contract', the application of which assumes a qualitative similarity between the corporation and a sovereign state.

The central relevance of the social contract approach can be stated in more analytical terms. If to speak of an *objective* implies the rationalisation of an interest in terms of the means available for achieving it, and an *interest* can be possessed only by a natural individual, it follows that to speak of the objective of a *legal* individual is to refer to the actual interests of the individuals it represents. Therefore, the objective of a business corporation as a legal individual must also be understood in terms of the individual interests it represents. Moreover, if the corporation is an individual under the law, then it pursues objectives legally *as if* it had an individual will. And as a being with an individual will cannot pursue two objectives simultaneously that are in contradiction, so too a corporation can have only one objective at any one time. As an objective implies an interest, a single objective for a multiplicity of individuals implies *unanimity* of interests among the individuals represented by the corporation. In analysing the corporate objective, this makes it crucial to answer the question: over how many individuals can the unanimity of interests extend for which the corporation can be the representative?[13] By viewing the corporation by analogy with a sovereign state, an association of all stakeholders with a unanimous interest in the corporation can be envisaged. The corporation would then represent in its objectives the combined interest of all the relevant stakeholders, however precisely these stakeholders are defined.

However, this chapter has argued that no such unanimity of interests exists amongst those groups commonly considered to be the stakeholders of an organisation. The philosophical arguments engaged with in Chapter 3, which posit a 'social contract' to form a state with physical

---

[13] In the case of shareholders, unanimity of interest will not necessarily mean that all desire identical outcomes from the corporation (e.g., some may prioritise capital gains, others dividends). Instead, it will consist in their agreement to entrust their investment to the control and discretion of management, subject to various constraints such as those provided by company law (e.g., the rules on the rights of minority shareholders).

powers of coercion over its subjects, cannot be applied to the modern business corporation without great difficulty and inconsistency. It can be concluded that on no voluntary grounds, and hence on no grounds that are consistent with the ethical framework of a market economy, can a corporation legitimately represent in its objectives the interests of any stakeholder other than the shareholders. Stakeholder theory is therefore incompatible with a concept of the corporation as a commercial entity and with the very existence of a market economy.

6 | *Shareholder theory and its limitations*

The previous chapters found no version of stakeholder theory that is compatible with the basic ethical framework of capitalism. This implies that the 'shareholder theory', of which a brief outline was given in Chapter 1, is the only perspective on corporate responsibility consistent with the context of a market economy. However, as also seen earlier, this perspective has been identified as the underlying cause of many of the corporate scandals of recent years. Various critics have seen the objective to maximise shareholder wealth as intrinsically linked to accounting scandals, environmental pollution, the exploitation of cheap labour, and other grievances widely held today against the corporation. I argued that the distinctive feature of stakeholder theory is its attempt to repudiate the shareholder view without altering the structure of a capitalist economy. Even if it ultimately fails in this attempt, an argument for the shareholder theory is clearly incomplete if it is unable to address the ethical concerns that led in the first place to the popularity of rival views. The aim of this chapter is to address this issue by examining the ethical limitations of the shareholder theory as well as how, in the context of the United Kingdom, these shortcomings might be mitigated by recent changes in company law.

The chapter begins by placing the argument developed here in the context of other attempts to refute stakeholder theory. I consider the different ways in which stakeholder theory has been rejected in favour of a corporate objective of profit maximisation, and make a distinction between arguments developed on *consequentialist* grounds and those that have a *deontological* basis.[1] This is to contrast arguments that appeal to the moral worth of the consequences expected from different kinds of corporate objective (Henderson, 2001; Jensen, 2002) with

---

At the time of going to press, a substantially revised version of this chapter was under review at the *Journal of Business Ethics*.

[1] Kaler (2006: 253) has a similar interpretation.

those holding that management is bound by a moral obligation *intrinsic* to the principal–agent relationship to further shareholder interests. This version of shareholder theory is best known in the form of Milton Friedman's (1962, 1970) criticisms of CSR, though more recent examples can be found in the work of Sternberg (2000, 2004) and Marcoux (2003).[2] This is also the form in which my argument has been made. However, as I will argue later, it need not be inconsistent with this ethical framework for managers to pursue objectives contrary to the maximisation of shareholder wealth.

The deontological shareholder theory is presented here as the most compelling account of the corporate objective in a market economy. However, I proceed to ask what *limitations* it has as an applied ethical theory. To do so I consider Immanuel Kant's moral philosophy in *The Metaphysics of Morals* (1797/1996).[3] Kant's theory suggests that contracts formed between a corporation and its various stakeholders have moral force because to breach a contract right is to violate the categorical imperative that human beings are treated always as an end and never merely as a means. However, this is to leave open the question of what ends a person has a duty to acquire through the exercise of the freedom that such rights protect. Kant demarcates a *perfect* duty to respect the rights of all others to pursue their ends from an *imperfect* duty to take as one's end the happiness of others. He calls the latter a 'duty of beneficence'.

In the case of corporations with dispersed ownership it can be argued, in keeping with the shareholder theory, that a perfect duty to treat all stakeholders as ends is consistent with Friedman's (1970) precept that a corporation is to honour contracts it has entered while avoiding deception and fraud. Such a responsibility fits with a view of the corporation as a 'network of contracts' and is consistent with legal enforcement. However, there remains the question of how managers can fulfil a contractual obligation to promote shareholder interests where these ought to comprise not merely financial gain but also the

---

[2] This description of a particular understanding of the manager–shareholder relationship relates simply to the Greek verb *dein* 'to bind' and is opposed to a strictly consequentialist understanding. It is not meant to imply a necessary connection to Kant's ethics. I do not suggest that the three authors taken here as exemplars of the deontological approach would identify themselves as Kantians.

[3] While Kant's arguments are not often directly appealed to in defences of the shareholder theory, the framework of his ideas is consistent with the deontological version of the theory. An analysis of Kant's arguments can therefore yield insights into the theory's limitations.

happiness and well-being of various non-shareholding stakeholders. Such a duty would be 'imperfect' and legally unenforceable because it entails a *voluntary* adoption of ends. In this case, how would a manager perceive the ends that shareholders wish to endorse? Even where such knowledge is present, there is the further difficulty that individual shareholders might support the pursuit of incompatible goals with the corporation's property.

It can be argued that the difficulty of reconciling what Kant calls 'imperfect duty' with the principal–agent relationship is at the basis of many of the contemporary ethical controversies that are thought to be the result of the shareholder theory. When Bakan (2004) describes the corporation as a 'pathological' institution which pursues its own interest relentlessly, it can be said that the corporation lends itself to such observations because of the split that occurs in practice between these two types of duty.

The separation of ownership and control

In enquiring into the content of a corporation's 'social responsibilities', specifically into whether its objectives are reducible to the interests of shareholders or a wider range of stakeholders, one can ask what distinguishes the business corporation from other kinds of market participant. Many reasons are offered for why the modern business corporation warrants an extra level of moral scrutiny from that which individuals normally receive. A range of ethical grievances can easily be listed in which the role of the business corporation is uniquely common. However, for writers who defend a 'shareholder theory' of the firm and offer a critique of CSR, what is typically considered to be the distinguishing feature of the corporation is the separation between the ownership and control of its assets.

In the landmark study of this phenomenon, Adolf Berle and Gardiner Means argue in *The Modern Corporation and Private Property* (1932) that not only had the corporation in the early 1930s come to play an unprecedented role in the economic life of American people, but also the separation of ownership from control would change fundamentally the way in which the economic organisation of society could be perceived. They write:

The translation of perhaps two-thirds of the industrial wealth of the country from individual ownership to ownership by the large, publicly financed

corporations vitally changes the lives of property owners, the lives of workers, and the methods of property tenure. The divorce of ownership from
control consequent on that process almost necessarily involves a new form
of economic organization of society. (1932: vii–viii)

They draw attention to how this separation between ownership and
control will create a situation in which the interests of the owner and
of the manager may diverge (1932: 6), a concern at the root of the
principal–agent problem still being discussed today. However, it is not
merely the difficulty of ensuring that managers act in the interest of
owners that leads Berle and Means to write that a new form of the economic organisation of society must be envisaged. It is because in their
view the deeply rooted understanding of a market economy in which
individuals acting rationally in their own self-interest will produce an
unintended yet maximally efficient social outcome, a view going back
at least to Adam Smith (1776/1970),[4] relies upon a crucial premise that
no longer holds. According to Berle and Means (1932: 8), ownership
of property in a free enterprise system had previously been assumed
to include 'full power of manual disposition with complete right to
enjoy the use, the fruits, and the proceeds of physical assets'. But there
has now resulted 'the dissolution of the old atom of ownership into its
component parts, control and beneficial ownership' (ibid.).

The significance of this, they argue, is that self-interest in using private property is no longer a guarantee of economic efficiency, because
in the publicly owned corporation the individual no longer has control
over his or her property and cannot use it directly in serving his or her
own interests. This means that:

The stockholders ... to whom the profits of the corporation go, cannot be
motivated by those profits to a more efficient use of the property, since they
have surrendered all disposition of it to those in control of the enterprise. The
explosion of the atom of property destroys the basis of the old assumption
that the quest for profits will spur the owner of industrial property to its

---

[4] As encapsulated in Smith's remark: 'm an has almost constant occasion for the
help of his brethren, and it is vain for him to expect it from their benevolence
only. He will be more likely to prevail if he can interest their self-love in his
favour, and show them that it is for their advantage to do for him what he
requires of them' (1776/1970: 118). As such, 'It is not from the benevolence of
the butcher, the brewer, or the baker that we expect our dinner, but from their
regard to their own interest' (1776/1970: 119).

effective use. It consequently challenges the fundamental economic principle of individual initiative in industrial enterprise. (1932: 9)

This argument seems to highlight the importance of studying how the gap between ownership and control can be bridged, or more particularly the mechanisms of governance by which agents can be held accountable to principals.[5] If mechanisms of accountability cannot be put in place that work effectively to ensure that the interests of owners are followed, then it can be argued that as long as the corporate form remains dominant, markets are not likely to work efficiently in transferring resources to where there is the greatest demand (which would supposedly be the case in a society of individuals trading to maximise personal profit), and total social utility will decline. Stated here in a simple form, this can be seen as the basis of the consequentialist defence of profit maximisation, in which stakeholder theory is argued to undermine the very possibility of corporate accountability with overall social utility (or welfare) suffering as a consequence.

In the context of corporate accountability, a large body of literature has developed in recent decades as a response to the principal–agent problem. Strong and Waterson summarise the basic assumptions underpinning the approaches taken so far:

The simplest agency model assumes that the principal delegates to the agent the responsibility for selecting and implementing an action. The agent is compensated by the principal, with the principal being the residual claimant to the outcome of the agent's act, after payment of compensation. The principal's problem is to negotiate a contract specifying the agent's remuneration, knowing that their interests are not in complete harmony.[6] (1987: 19–20)

Various responses include that of Alchian and Demsetz (1972), for whom the key difficulty in any business organisation is monitoring inputs and matching them to rewards. This is because in team-based

---

[5] Putterman and Krozsner (1996: 13), in their overview of theories concerning the economic nature of the firm, write: 'The principal-agent framework also plays a central role in several of the analyses of management incentives and accountability stimulated by the Berle and Means conception of "separation of ownership and control"'. See also Clarke and McGuiness (1987: 4) for a similar observation of the link between Berle and Means (1932) and the 'principal-agent' problem.

[6] A very similar interpretation can be found near the start of Jensen and Meckling's (1976: 309) famous article *Theory of the Firm: Managerial Behaviour, Agency Costs and Ownership Structure*.

production, which for them is the distinguishing feature of a firm, the contribution made by each team member is not easy to isolate: 'it is difficult, solely by observing total output, to either define or determine *each* individual's contribution to this output' (1972: 779). They raise the question of who will monitor the monitor who is assigned the task of measuring inputs and allocating rewards to members of the team; what is to stop the monitor from 'shirking' and presenting the firm with an ever-recurring agency problem? The solution they suggest is to 'give him [the monitor] title to the net earnings of the team, net of payments to other inputs. If owners of cooperating inputs agree with the monitor that he is to receive any residual product... the monitor will have an added incentive not to shirk as a monitor' (1972: 782).

For Alchian and Demsetz (1972: 786), the monitor, who 'hires, fires, changes, promotes, and renegotiates', should be the residual claimant, or 'one whose pay or reward is more than any others correlated with fluctuations in the residual value of the firm'. This is a way in which the split between ownership and control can be bridged, by ensuring that the rewards given to those who control the firm are in close proportion to its residual value, and therefore consistent with the interests of owners.

Another notable approach is the transaction cost theory pioneered in recent years by Oliver Williamson (1975, 1985), building on the work of Ronald Coase (1937). Williamson's theory has already been commented upon in Chapter 2. As with Alchian and Demsetz (1972), he argues that it is economically efficient to allow those in a corporation who bear a residual risk, who lack an *ex ante* contractible fixed claim on the firm, to be responsible for the governance of that firm (or for appointing managers on their behalf). Williamson (1985: 304, 324) gives various reasons that shareholders alone should be considered the bearers of residual risk, in virtue of the unique level of transaction-specific risk in their investments, and other investors such as customers and employees do not bear this same risk. The implication, he argues, is that only shareholders should have direct involvement in the governance of a corporation.

While these different approaches are passed over briefly, they clearly all represent sustained attempts to address the implications of the dissolution of the 'old atom of property' identified by Berle and Means (1932). These theories are potential solutions to the removal of the vital premise in arguments connecting self-interested profit-seeking behaviour with market efficiency and social welfare: the role of rational self-interest in the direct use of private property.

At this point, the connection between the separation of ownership and control and the question of a corporation's social responsibilities can be brought into clearer focus. In most of the well-known theoretical solutions to the agency problem (including those outlined in the preceding), the position is taken that management should be directly accountable only to those who hold a residual risk in the firm, and the bearers of this risk are argued to be the shareholders. Alchian and Demsetz (1972: 788) write: 'The corporate stockholders retain the authority to revise membership of the management group and over major decisions that affect the structure of the corporation or its dissolution'. A similar insistence on shareholder authority can be seen in Jensen and Meckling (1976) and Williamson (1985).[7]

However, one of the questions raised by Berle and Means (1932) is whether the separation of ownership and control negates what they call the 'traditional logic of property', together with the implication that a firm should be run in the interests of its owners. Instead, they suggest that the interests of the wider community might now be given priority:

The extensive separation of ownership and control, and the strengthening of the powers of control, raise a new situation calling for a decision whether social and legal pressure should be applied in an effort to insure corporate operation primarily in the interests of the 'owners' or whether such pressure shall be applied in the interests of some other or wider group. (1932: 333)

They argue that under the traditional logic of property, the owner of industrial property would have been entitled to all the accretions in its value (1932: 334). The powers of control can be considered powers in *trust*: 'The controlling group is, in form at least, managing and controlling a corporation for the benefit of the owners' (1932: 335). However, they claim that the traditional theory of property is no longer valid because in the modern corporation *active* property has become separated from *passive* property, so that the owners still have use of property in stock but not in the instruments of production (1932: 347).

---

[7] Sundaram and Inkpen (2004: 352) observe that Alchian and Demsetz (1972) and Jensen and Meckling (1976) were seen as bolstering the attack on CSR initiated by Friedman (1970).

For them the possibility exists that owners of passive property, such as shareholders of corporations, have surrendered control and responsibility of the active property and so have given up the right for it to be run in their sole interest: 'they have released the community from the obligation to protect them to the full extent implied in the doctrine of strict property rights' (1932: 355). In arguing that the surrender of active property diminishes the right of private ownership over that property, Berle and Means do not imply that *controllers* of this property are at liberty to use it for their own ends. Instead, they assert: 'The control groups have, rather, cleared the way for the claims of a group far wider than either the owners or the control. They have placed the community in a position to demand that the modern corporation serve not alone the owners or the control but all society' (1932: 355–6). The interests of the community (whatever these might be) are said to have priority over the interests of both controllers and owners.

The consequentialist critique of stakeholder theory

If the separation of ownership and control in the modern corporation opens up two important questions, one being whether the role of self-interest in the use of property can any longer be a guarantee of economic efficiency, and the other whether the active use of corporate property has been surrendered to the interests of the community, it is as a response to both these questions that the consequentialist critique of stakeholder theory is made. It is held that the risk posed to economic efficiency and overall social utility by the separation of ownership and control is of fundamental importance from a moral perspective. As writers such as Jensen (2002) and Henderson (2001) argue, the only way to mitigate this risk is by holding managers as agents directly accountable to shareholders as principals. Stakeholder theory is to be deplored because it undermines this solution.

Jensen (2002) and Henderson (2001) suggest that management cannot act as if it is accountable to all stakeholders and expect the market value of the firm to be at its maximum. In turn, they reason that if the value of the firm is not being maximised and profits are not the firm's single objective, then overall social welfare will decline. Henderson (2001: 58) writes: 'embracing CSR would inevitably have consequences that would raise the cost of doing business, could well reduce revenues, and might also cause companies to sponsor low-yielding investments which they would otherwise have turned down'. Henderson challenges the assumption that the adoption of CSR (or stakeholder theory) by a business will make for long-term profitability. This claim he believes is dubious: 'It rests on the twin premises that the doctrine of CSR mirrors "society's expectations" ... and that the extent to which a company meets these expectations will now determine its profitability ... both premises are open to question. In some respects the doctrine of CSR will tend to reduce profits, perhaps significantly' (2001: 75).

If there is no direct link between the pursuit of stakeholder objectives and profit maximisation, then if one accepts the role of the latter in producing economic efficiency (an understanding which Berle and Means (1932: 9) suggest has stood as the foundation of the economic order of society for three hundred years), the consequentialist objection to stakeholder theory now appears in full view. Jensen declares emphatically that

200 years' worth of work in economics and finance indicate that social welfare is maximised when all firms in an economy maximise total firm value. The intuition behind this criterion is simply that (social) value is created when a firm produces an output or set of outputs that are valued by its customers at more than the value of the inputs it consumes. (2002: 239)

He states that 'a firm taking inputs out of the economy and putting its output of goods and services back into the economy increases aggregate welfare if the prices at which it sells the goods more than cover the costs it incurs in purchasing the inputs' and for this reason 'profit maximisation leads to an efficient social outcome' (2002: 240). It follows that if agents can be held accountable to principals for maximising the total firm value, then the concern raised by Berle and Means (1932) of the decline of social welfare caused by the split between passive and active property, can (by their own logic) be solved.[8] If stakeholder

---

[8] Given the insights of 'behavioural finance', it can be objected that a firm's value as measured by its share price is determined primarily by investor perception and market psychology, and these will not always adhere to 'economic fundamentals' such as the present value of a firm's future cash flows (see Dembinski, 2009: 90). Jensen would presumably respond that society is better off when firm value is understood in terms of economic fundamentals rather than short-term investor perception. He writes: 'It is possible for markets not

theory, or CSR, would not offer management any such objective, then the single criterion of profit maximisation is arguably an ethically superior alternative, on the consequential grounds that it must lead to higher overall social welfare. For this reason, Henderson writes: 'I believe that the adoption of CSR would make people in general worse off, and that it could be especially damaging for the economic prospects of poor countries' (2001: 155).

The reason that it is argued stakeholder theory fails is not merely that it compels business to pursue goals other than profit maximisation, leading to a Pareto-inefficient use of resources and diminution of social welfare. It is asserted that for a company to pursue any objective such as 'maximising profits', an effective mechanism of *accountability* must be in place to ensure that managers carry this out and are rewarded in accordance with their success in achieving it. This can be seen as the aim of the various agency theories discussed earlier. However, its opponents argue that stakeholder theory leaves a business with no single objective, and therefore makes any system of accountability inherently unfeasible. The notion that management can respond effectively to multiple accountabilities, or take a 'multi-fiduciary' approach to running a business, has come under attack from a number of authors.

Bainbridge (1993), Henderson (2001), Jensen (2001), Sternberg (2004) and Sundaram and Inkpen (2004) emphasise the managerial confusion and/or lack of accountability that would result from an attempt to run a business in the interests of all stakeholders. Jensen (2001) believes that effectively stakeholder theory asks managers to maximise the performance of the firm in more than one dimension, but this is 'logically impossible' because 'purposeful behaviour requires a single valued objective function' (2001: 6). Jensen (2001) thinks that this objective ought to be to maximise the total value of the firm, and he argues that 'stakeholder theory should not be viewed as a legitimate contender to value maximisation because it fails to provide a complete

to know the full implications of a firm's policies until they begin to show up in cash flows over time. In such a case, the firm must lead the market to understand the full value implications of its policies, then wait for the market to catch up and recognize the real value of its decisions... Value creation does not mean succumbing to the vagaries of the movements in a firm's value from day to day. The market is inevitably ignorant of many managerial actions and opportunities, at least in the short-run. It is the job of directors, managers, and employees to resist the temptation to conform to the pressures of equity and debt markets' (2002: 246).

specification of the corporate purpose or objective function' (2001: 9). Why might this be problematic? Bainbridge (1993) draws attention to the problem of serving 'two masters'. He asks 'whose interests should management pursue when shareholder and non-shareholder interests are in irreconcilable conflict?' (1993: 1435). Likewise, for Sundaram and Inkpen (2004: 354), 'A basic problem with the stakeholder view is that the question of which stakeholder should matter is left unanswered. To suggest that managers must juggle multiple goals in a complex hierarchy is wishful thinking'. Without a determinate objective for the firm, it is feared that management will not know which stakeholder to respond to when interests conflict.

These authors and others argue that the 'logical impossibility' with which management is faced under a stakeholder approach leads to confusion and unaccountability, and ultimately this plays into the hands of managerial self-interest. Jensen (2002: 238) writes that stakeholder theory 'leaves the manager with no objective. The result will be confusion and lack of purpose'. The point is that this confusion can only arise because managers are not strictly accountable to anyone, which in effect gives them free rein to do as they choose with corporate assets. Jensen articulates this as follows:

With no criteria for performance, managers cannot be evaluated in any principled way. Therefore, stakeholder theory plays into the hands of self-interested managers allowing them to pursue their own interests at the expense of society and the firm's financial claimants. It allows managers and directors to invest in their favourite projects that destroy firm-value whatever they are (the environment, art, cities, medical research) without having to justify the value destruction. (2002: 242)

This has the effect of politicising the corporation because it 'leaves its managers empowered to exercise their own preferences in spending the firm's resources' (2002: 237).

Bainbridge (1993: 1438) offers the similar insight that 'management could freely pursue its own self-interest by playing shareholders off against non-shareholders.' Management could do this, he writes, by justifying any self-serving action by representing it in terms of stakeholder benefits. The same view is asserted by Sternberg (2004: 135), who writes: 'An organisation that is accountable to everyone, is actually accountable to no one: accountability that is diffuse, is effectively non-existent'. This leads Sternberg to conclude that managers 'are effectively left free to pursue their own arbitrary ends. Accordingly, stakeholder theory gives full rein to arrogant and unresponsive managements, and to extravagance in respect of salaries, perks and premises' (ibid.). Williamson (1985: 311), in criticising the idea of board representation for 'constituencies' other than shareholders, writes of the serious prospect that 'the inclusion of partisan constituencies on the board invites opportunism' and that 'corporate assets may be dissipated in the support of "worthy causes" with which specialized constituencies sympathize'.

The concern that stakeholder theory undermines accountability is clearly pervasive. If Berle and Means (1932: 355–6) anticipate a certain version of CSR in their claim that the interests of the community should take priority over those of owners, then the ironic implication of the arguments cited above is that such an endorsement of CSR would *exacerbate* the decline in social utility caused by the separation of ownership and control, identified in the first place by Berle and Means (1932: 9). This is because it subverts any system of accountability that might bridge this separation.

Criticisms of this sort have drawn a mixed response from stakeholder theorists. Phillips (2003) argues that the agency-based criticism is 'the result of the overextended metaphor of agency theory in economics. If managers are agents or fiduciaries at all, it is to the *organization* and not to the shareowners' (2003: 19). Phillips argues that the corporation is an entity in itself, in that it can enter contracts and own property, and has standing in a court of law. He maintains that the obligations of managers run directly to the organisation itself, and not to any particular stakeholder group. There is an agency relationship of sorts, therefore, but shareholders are not the sole beneficiary. Phillips writes: 'Top managers are agents for the corporation, which is not merely a shorthand way of saying that they are agents for the shareholders. The corporation is meaningfully distinct' (2003: 20).

The first question that suggests itself here is how the 'organisation' can hold management to account, while being independent of the interests of actual stakeholder groups. Second, even if management can be held accountable to the abstract entity, the 'organisation', how is management to know what the objectives of the organisation are, independent of the interests of particular stakeholders? If the objectives that the organisation can pursue are not in fact separable from the interests of the various investors in that organisation, then if these various interests have the potential to conflict (e.g., the interest of employees in a pay rise versus the desire of shareholders for a higher dividend) then the criticism still stands that stakeholder theory leaves management unaccountable, unless it can specify *which* stakeholders should be responded to and *what* the corporate objective should be.

A further rebuttal to the charge of managerial unaccountability from Phillips (2003: 20) and Freeman et al. (2004: 366) is that managerial opportunism is just as evident under the shareholder approach. They point to the accounting scandals of Enron and WorldCom as examples and criticise the notion that management should have a single objective to guide their day-to-day activities, arguing that accountability will actually work better when management is held to account by many stakeholder groups instead of just one (Phillips 2003: 21). Phillips admits that 'Stakeholder theory does fail to provide an algorithm for day-to-day managerial decision making, due to the level of abstraction at which the discussion is taking place' (2003: 22). However, 'the same critique may be levelled at the conventional shareholder-centred view. The managerial dictate to maximize shareholder wealth stands mute when queried, How? This is because of the innumerable ways to do so' (2003: 23). Likewise, Freeman et al. (2004: 366) argue: 'The problem with focusing on a single objective is that the world is complex, and managers and directors are boundedly rational' and make the observation that: 'It has long been known in philosophy, at least since John Stuart Mill and probably since Aristotle, that if you want to maximize a particular thing, such as utility, you should perhaps not try to do it consciously. As Hayek and others have suggested, in a complex world order emerges' (2004: 367).

However, this does not appear to be an argument against a firm having a single objective. To say that certain objectives can best be achieved through indirect means, perhaps because of bounded rationality, as in Mill's (1861/1991) discussion of the ordinary rules of morality as a better guide for maximising utility than trying to calculate the utility of every act, or Hayek's (1988) suggestion that the direct pursuit of our particular objectives leads to a greater overall social gain if done in accordance with unconsciously developed rules rather than a consciously designed system, is *not* to say it is better for a person (or corporation) to pursue *multiple* objectives simultaneously instead of a single one. Kaler (2006), who is sympathetic to some aspects of stakeholder theory, writes, 'there is a crucial difference between that meeting of multiple demands as a means to the end of serving just one required by the stockholder approach to running companies and that meeting of multiple demands as an end in itself required by the stakeholder approach' (2006: 262). He adds that the complexity of the first approach is simply 'the possibility of many different aids and impediments to the achievement of an objective. Complexity of the second kind is that possibility with respect to *multiple* objectives' (ibid., emphasis in original). Consequently, 'implementation of a stakeholder approach to running companies is always going to be a more complex affair than implementation of its stockholder alternative' (2006: 262–3).

At this stage, it is important to note that Jensen's well-known critique of stakeholder theory is not a defence of the orthodox view that the sole aim of a firm should be to further the interests of shareholders. Instead, the objective of a corporation should be that which makes the greatest contribution to the general welfare of society. Jensen (2002: 239) poses the question of whether shareholders should hold a privileged position over other constituencies such as employees, customers and creditors, and writes, 'it is both unproductive and incorrect to frame the issue in this manner. The real issue is what firm behaviour will result in the least social waste, or equivalently, what behaviour will get the most out of society's limited resources'. In a later article, Jensen asserts:

Stockholder value maximization has been wrong from the social viewpoint from the start. There is nothing special about stockholders in the firm . . . it is time we take it as given that maximizing the value of a firm's equity will not produce maximum value of the firm as a whole. And it will certainly not produce maximum value for society. (2008: 167)

Jensen believes that an objective of long-term profit maximisation also maximises 'the sum of the market values of equity, debt, and any other contingent claims outstanding on the firm' (2002: 239), and in turn the firm is argued to create the highest possible 'social' value, for the reasons given earlier. Jensen articulates his normative position as follows: 'I have argued positively that if firms follow value creation, social welfare will be greater and normatively that this is desirable' (2002: 255). Long-term share value is merely one determinant among others of long-term firm value, and 'stock-holders are not some special constituency that ranks above all others' (2002: 246).

In fact, the objective of maximising total firm value through a focus on long-term profit is not inconsistent with the arguments of stakeholder theorists such as Sacconi (2004) and Phillips (2003) who oppose the shareholder view. Sacconi (2004), whose Rawlsian version of CSR was outlined in Chapter 2, recognises the problem of accountability and attempts to solve it. Sacconi considers Jensen's objections explicitly, and finds that they do not apply to his defence of CSR. He writes that his theory 'by no means ignores the existence of a distributive conflict, but instead resolves it by identifying a bargaining equilibrium that permits mutual cooperation among the members of the team' (2004: 17). This bargaining equilibrium, as seen earlier, can be achieved from behind a hypothetical 'veil of ignorance' resulting in a 'social contract' between all stakeholders of a firm. This means that 'we can simply substitute profit maximisation with maximisation of the function which assigns the solution to the bargaining game and assume this as the firm's (perfectly computable) objective-function' (2004: 17–18).

Through this bargaining equilibrium the potential for a conflict between stakeholder interests is hypothetically removed. Furthermore, he suggests in his paper that rational wealth-maximising stakeholders would desire the overall value of the firm to be at its maximum, which provides exactly the same objective function that Jensen (2002) propounds. So in response to Jensen and other critics one could postulate a corporate arrangement where all stakeholders desire the value of the firm to be maximised, and the distribution between wages, dividends, interest on loans, etc., could then be decided, for example (as in Sacconi 2004), by devising a fair outcome to a hypothetical bargaining process. This seems to be the position taken by Phillips, who writes that 'stakeholder theory, when applied to for-profit business organizations, is consistent with profit maximization. Let us distinguish, however, between profitability and *maximizing shareholder wealth* . . . Maximizing profit says nothing about who gets a say in the decision making or who gets how much of this value, so maximized' (2003: 24, emphasis in original). In theory an organisation could be run with the objective of maximising profits, but be held accountable by all stakeholders for distributing this profit in accordance with the interests of all relevant stakeholders, with none having priority over another.

In theory, at least, answers have been given to the charge of unaccountability made by many critics of the stakeholder approach. What they suggest is that if the critique is based merely on the need to hold managers accountable for profit maximisation (because this is instrumental in producing higher levels of social welfare), then this is indistinguishable from stakeholder theory if the latter holds management accountable for the *same* objective. To this objective, stakeholder theorists add a distributional qualification to meet the legitimate needs of stakeholders. However, beyond profit maximisation, the consequentialist theory does not seem to answer the question of whether or how profits might be distributed among stakeholders, or *why* management should be accountable to one group rather than another for achieving corporate objectives.

It therefore seems that the shareholder view has received a more consistent defence in the deontological arguments of Milton Friedman (1962, 1970). Unlike the consequentialist critique of CSR, Friedman attempts to justify the standing of shareholders as the one group in whose interests a corporation must be run. By looking at the moral obligations that arise directly out of the contractual nature of the firm, in the context of the property rights recognised as essential in a market economy, the accountability of agents for the maximisation of shareholder value receives a justification without the contingencies of the consequentialist view.

The deontological defence of shareholder theory

The deontological variant of shareholder theory is epitomised in a famous quotation from Milton Friedman's *Capitalism and Freedom* (1962: 133), repeated in a later article for the *New York Times* magazine (1970): 'there is one and only one social responsibility of business – to use its resources and engage in activities designed to increase its profits so long as it stays within the rules of the game, which is to say, engages in open and free competition without deception and fraud'.

Given the extent to which this statement has a central place in debates surrounding the shareholder theory, and its exemplification of the deontological version of the theory formulated here, it is useful to carry out an analysis of Friedman's argument before the limitations of shareholder theory are explored in the next section. To appreciate the reasoning behind this statement, one must first consider the ethical and political principles that reinforce 'the rules of the game'. Friedman's work can be seen as part of a libertarian tradition that emphasises the inviolability of individuals and the need for clear boundaries protecting them from illegitimate coercion. There is a resemblance between the ethical principles on which he defends capitalism and the libertarianism of Robert Nozick (1974) in *Anarchy, State and Utopia*.

Friedman's objections to CSR can be deduced from his broader libertarian principles. He argues that government action is appropriate where its goal is to minimise the costs of 'neighbourhood effects'[9] and technical monopolies (1962: 27), maintain a monetary system, and supplement the work of private charities and families in protecting the irresponsible (1962: 34). However, further government activity is required only if it aims at 'the maintenance of law and order to prevent physical coercion of one individual by another and to enforce contracts voluntarily entered into, thus giving substance to "private"' (1962: 14). As will be seen later, the ethical status of contracts voluntarily reached between individuals is an essential part of his criticism of corporate social responsibility. To see why this is the case, it is crucial to observe that Friedman's concept of a free individual includes the right to own personal property:

In an ideal free market resting on private property, no individual can coerce any other, all cooperation is voluntary, all parties to such cooperation benefit or they need not participate. There are no 'social' values, no 'social' responsibilities in any sense other than the shared values and responsibilities of individuals. Society is a collection of individuals and of the various groups they voluntarily form. (1970)

From the above arguments, two moral principles can be derived on the basis of which Friedman's 'shareholder theory' can logically be defended. First, individuals have the right to use their freedom in accordance with any ends of their choice, provided that they do not encroach upon the freedom of others to do the same. Second, the right to own property is intrinsic to the concept of a free individual. Individuals ought therefore to possess the liberty to use their property within the constraints set by the first principle. This is of course to simplify Friedman's standpoint, but these principles clarify the grounds of his argument against CSR. His assumption of property rights is consistent with the ethical principles held in Chapter 4 to be indispensable for a

---

[9] Otherwise known as 'externalities'.

market economy. It was argued there that if trade is a rational activity aimed at the satisfaction of one's ends, then one must possess a right to ownership of the fruits of trade. Nevertheless, it is still to be seen how these principles lead to the argument that the only responsibility of business is to increase its profits.

As the free choice of the individual is central to his ethical principles, Friedman holds that 'corporate' social responsibility is, strictly speaking, a misnomer. Only an individual can be the bearer of responsibility (1970). In keeping with an acceptance of the right to own property as part of the concept of a free individual, Friedman argues that it belongs to shareholders as owners of a corporation to determine its purposes:

> In a free enterprise, private-property system a corporate executive is an employee of the owners of the business. He has direct responsibility to his employers. That responsibility is to conduct the business in accordance with their desires, which will generally be to make as much money as possible ... Of course, in some cases his employers may have a different objective. (1970)

Shareholders as owners are therefore considered to employ the managers of a corporation as agents to act in their interests. Here a deontological obligation arising from the contract between managers and shareholders is clearly assumed.

Friedman's 'shareholder theory' is therefore based upon three assumptions: there exists an individual right to the ownership of property; shareholders own the assets of a corporation in the same manner in which an individual owns personal property; and the relationship between shareholders and management is a contract in which control of the owners' property is delegated to the management. It follows that the fundamental responsibility of those running a business is to further the interests of the property owners. This will usually entail making profit the substantive objective of business activity.[10]

---

[10] This is not to assume that the maximisation of shareholder value and maximisation of profits are identical. See Sternberg (2000: 42–9) for a discussion of how 'owner value' can be distinguished from other objectives associated with shareholder interests, such as profits, wealth, 'added value' and share price.

Again, the principles invoked by Friedman are consistent with those defended in Chapter 4. Besides a right to property, it was argued that the rational expectations established through the interpersonal activity of trade imply a right of *contract* as an essential principle of a market economy. Furthermore, it was held that the only stakeholders with a logical claim to 'ownership' of the corporation are the shareholders, though few shareholder theorists have seen the need to defend this point explicitly. At its inception, a corporation comes to embody the interests of an association of property holders, and these interests cannot be those of any stakeholder group that trades with the corporation. Two subjective values for the good being traded would not exist and a necessary condition of trade would not be fulfilled. If shareholders delegate authority to management rather than entering into direct acts of exchange with the corporation, then the shareholders must be the association of property holders whose interests the corporation represents.

A recent exposition of the deontological approach, consistent with the principles set out here, can be found in the work of Elaine Sternberg (2000, 2004). In her book, *Just Business* (2000: 41), Sternberg writes that Friedman has been far too polite in castigating CSR as 'socialism', in fact: 'Using business resources for non-business purposes is tantamount to *theft*: an unjustified appropriation of the owners' property. Managers who employ business funds for anything other than the legitimate business objective are simply embezzling'[11] (emphasis in original). In her later book *Corporate Governance: Accountability in the Market Place*, her argument for the rights of shareholders is again consistent with the principles defended here. She writes: 'Although members of society do not lose whatever natural and legal rights

---

[11] In *Just Business* (2000) Sternberg employs an Aristotelian style of argument to demonstrate that the 'legitimate business objective' is that which is consistent with the essence of business, which she defines as the maximisation of long-term owner value (2000: 48–9). In this sense it is more correct to describe her argument as teleological, in fact she criticises stakeholder theory for 'the logical offence of teleopathy: in diverting funds from strictly business objectives to other purposes, they [managers] are pursuing the wrong ends' (2000: 42). However, her argument in favour of shareholder theory would be tautological if it started from the premise that the essence of business is to maximise owner value; the actual argument she gives, in terms of property rights and contractual obligations, is consistent with what is here referred to as the deontological approach.

they already have by becoming stakeholders of corporations, the only rights that they have in their capacity as stakeholders are those conferred on them by law or specific contractual agreements' (2004: 35). One of these natural rights is a property right, which must be upheld in the contractual relations that stakeholders enter into with the firm. This includes the contractual relation between shareholders and management. She later argues that 'stakeholder theory undermines two of the most fundamental features that characterise modern society: private property and the duties that agents owe to principals. The stakeholder doctrine undermines private property, because it denies owners the right to determine how their property will be used' (2004: 147). This resonates with the claim of Goodpaster (1991: 68) that 'the conscience of the corporation is a logical and moral extension of the consciences of its principals'.

A further important argument for the shareholder theory with a deontological basis is that of Marcoux (2003). He argues that the nature of a fiduciary relationship is such that it necessitates the impartial treatment of one stakeholder over another. As stakeholder theory demands that fiduciary duties are owed to *multiple* stakeholders, it in fact destroys the very possibility of fiduciary obligations in business (2003: 2). Marcoux writes: 'As stakeholder theory demands that the interests of all stakeholders be counted, and presumably served equally (i.e., non-partially) in the governance of the firm, and as fiduciary duties require partiality toward the interests of some (the beneficiaries) over others, it follows that stakeholder theory is non-fiduciary in character' (2003: 4).

Marcoux proceeds to identify the relationship between managers and shareholders as being fiduciary in nature, because of the vulnerability of shareholders' investments. As responsibilities that are morally binding in themselves are basic to any fiduciary relationship, he concludes that the only objective management can be morally bound to follow is to act in the interests of shareholders alone. In explaining that the obligations here are not derived consequentially but are intrinsic to the 'moral core of fiduciary relations', Marcoux writes that 'it is something about *me*, and something about *my* situation, that would make the failure to exercise fiduciary duties morally wrong' (2003: 10, emphasis in original). He continues: 'Though collaterally this may affect society as a whole, the effect is only collateral. The moral wrongness of subordinating the interests of the

beneficiary exists quite apart from the aggregate effects on society'
(ibid.).

The limits of contractual duties

In the context of the principles discussed in the preceding, the deontological defence of the shareholder view can be seen to have its starting
point in the equality of rights possessed by all individuals, simply
in their capacity as human beings. This idea is central to most of
contemporary libertarian theory, for example in the opening line of
Robert Nozick's (1974) *Anarchy, State and Utopia*: 'Individuals have
rights, and there are things that no group or individual may do to them
(without violating their rights)' (1974: ix). This implies not merely that
shareholders have entitlements with respect to a firm, but that *all* stakeholders as individuals have rights that must be respected. This version
of shareholder theory therefore assumes that the managers of a corporation are constrained by a set of rights held equally by all, whether
these concern contractual responsibilities to shareholders or a range
of basic rights held by all stakeholders. The role-specific obligation of
managers to prioritise the interests of shareholders can be deduced
from the same argument: contractual rights would be infringed if
managers pursued 'socially responsible' causes without shareholder
approval.

According to this line of argument, managers have a contractual
responsibility to promote the 'desires' or 'wishes' of shareholders, yet
such a statement begs the question of whether managers possess the
requisite knowledge. Can a manager always be assumed to know what
the interests of shareholders are? Friedman (1970) asserts that to conduct business in the interests of shareholders will generally mean 'to
make as much money as possible while conforming to the basic rules of
the society, both those embodied in law and those embodied in ethical
custom'. Friedman concedes that in some instances the shareholders
may have a different objective: 'A group of persons might establish a
corporation for an eleemosynary purpose – for example, a hospital or a
school. The manager of such a corporation will not have money profit
as his objective but the rendering of certain services' (ibid.). His point
is that managers should pursue those objectives that are consistent
with the purposes for which a corporation is established. However,
he assumes that unless a corporation is created with a purpose other

than the pursuit of profit, managers should generally consider profit maximisation to be their principal goal. A similar position is taken by Sternberg, who asks:

What if owners want something other than maximum financial value from their enterprises? Examples are not hard to find. 'Ethical investment' is becoming more prominent, and firms have increasingly been stressing their explicitly non-financial aims... Owners are perfectly entitled to devote their organisations to all sorts of ends. To the extent that they pursue something other than maximum long-term value, however, they are simply not engaging in business. (2000: 44–5)

Any organisation established for the purpose of 'business' is therefore solely concerned with the maximisation of owner value, understood as the 'present value of the future cash flows that the owners will obtain from the business' (Sternberg 2000: 48). While Sternberg and Friedman acknowledge that organisations can of course be set up for all sorts of other purposes, they assume that the owners of business corporations want the value of their investment maximised indefinitely. They do not consider the ethical circumstances in which the owners may wish to deviate, if only briefly, from this central purpose.

At this juncture the relevance of Immanuel Kant's distinction between 'perfect' and 'imperfect' duties is apparent. His argument suggests that the moral obligations of management to shareholders are not captured entirely by a contractual responsibility to maximise the value of their investment. In discussing the principles of political 'right' (*Recht*),[12] which provide the ethical conditions for a state to exercise force over its citizens, Kant writes: 'Strict right rests... on the principle of its being possible to use external constraint that can coexist with the freedom of everyone in accordance with universal laws' (1797/1996: 25). As every person has an innate right to freedom (1797/1996: 30) because of the categorical imperative that people are to be treated always as an end and never merely as a means, it is possible for an external law (juridical rather than moral) to be applied universally in ensuring that one's external actions are in harmony with the freedom of all. This is not to say that the inner duty to obey the *moral* law (which is internal to a person's own conscience) can be replaced or

---

[12] According to Kant's translator Mary Gregor, he uses this term to refer to a 'system of external laws', rather than conformity to law (*recht* as an adjective), or simply 'a right' (*Recht* in its substantive use) (Gregor 199: xxxiv–xxxv).

alleviated through conformity to external law, but only that it is possible for a coercive law ensuring conformity with the freedom of all to apply with equal validity to all. In other words, a universal principle exists upon which any legislation can be based.

For this reason Kant says that 'duties of right' are capable of external lawgiving (1797/1996: 31). A 'duty of right' has the form of a 'perfect' duty to oneself and to others, which involves 'The right of humanity in our own person' and 'the right of human beings' (1797/1996: 32). That this sort of right is consistent with the deontological shareholder theory is suggested when Kant writes that the concept of 'right' concerns not the will of one person and the desires of another (so welfare/benevolence is not part of the concept) but only the relationship between the will of the first and the *choice* of the second (1797/1996: 24). An example of this is a 'contract right' whereby, as was seen earlier, 'what belongs to the promisor does not pass to the promisee (as acceptant) by the *separate* will of either but only by the *united will* of both' (1797/1996: 57–8, emphases in original). The contractual obligation held to exist between managers and shareholders falls under what Kant calls the concept of right, and can in theory be enforced by an external law, which is indeed what happens when managers are held legally accountable to their shareholders.

However, besides duties of right, Kant also identifies 'duties of virtue'. While the form of such virtues can be known objectively, the content for any single person is an internal matter for his or her conscience and cannot admit of a universal principle. It therefore cannot be enforced by an external law. For Kant, an 'imperfect' duty of virtue is directed to 'the end of human beings' (their own happiness) (1797/1996: 32). The reason that this form of duty cannot be enforced in line with a universal principle is that it involves a choice of *ends*, a choice which is necessarily an internal act of mind (1797/1996: 31), and cannot be prescribed for all human beings alike. Furthermore, the very act of *choosing* an end is part of the concept of an 'end' (an object of choice), for the pursuit of which one can take responsibility. The pursuit of an end cannot be *enforced* by a law external to a person's own conscience.

According to Kant, a duty to further the ends of others is a duty to make their happiness one's own end, but not their 'perfection', as this is something that a person has to seek in his or her own way as a duty to himself or herself which cannot overlap with the duty of another.

In explaining why one has a duty to pursue the happiness of others, Kant argues:

> The reason that it is a duty to be beneficent is this: since our self-love cannot be separated from our need to be loved (helped in case of need) by others as well, we therefore make ourselves an end for others; and the only way this maxim can be binding is through its qualification as a universal law, hence through our will to make others our end as well. The happiness of others is therefore an end that is also a duty. (1797/1996: 155–6)

However, Kant emphasises that in the case of a determinate action, it is impossible to say in accordance with a universal principle the *extent* to which the duty must be acted upon:

> It is impossible to assign determinate limits to the extent of this sacrifice. How far it should extend depends, in large part, on what each person's true needs are in view of his sensibilities, and it must be left to each to decide this for himself. For, a maxim of promoting others' happiness at the sacrifice of one's own happiness, one's true needs, would conflict with itself if it were made a universal law. Hence this duty is a *wide* one; the duty has in it a latitude for doing more or less, and no specific limits can be assigned to what should be done. (1797/1996: 156)

The indefinite range of this duty is another reason that it cannot be enforced through the rule of law, as the same law would not be equally applicable to all. Kant (1797/1996: 200–1) makes this clear when speaking of the injunction to 'love your *neighbour* (your fellow man) as yourself'. He argues: 'I cannot, without contradicting myself, say that I ought to love every human being as myself, since the measure of self-love would allow for no difference in degree'. As regards benevolence in my *wishes* I can take delight in the well-being of every other, but as regards 'active, practical benevolence (beneficence), making the well being and happiness of others my *end*... I can, without violating the universality of the maxim, vary the degree greatly in accordance with the different objects of my love (one of whom concerns me more closely than another)' (ibid., emphases in original).

If the duty to further the ends of others is indeterminate in any given case, being contingent upon the 'sensibilities' that a person has with regard to particular objects and the extent to which his or her own needs are satisfied, then an important question is posed for the agency relationship between managers and shareholders. Shareholders might establish a company with the general aim of maximising the long-term value of their investment, with the objects of the company clearly set out in the memorandum of association. However, on this basis alone, managers cannot infer how shareholders may wish their investment to be spent in particular circumstances in which a 'duty of virtue' (to use Kant's term) is apparent. The duty of virtue is not incumbent upon managers themselves, as the assets of the company are not their property to use in accordance with ends of their choice. They have a contractual obligation (a 'duty of right') to use the property in accordance with the ends of shareholders. However, where a duty to serve the well-being of any particular stakeholder is present, how is a manager to gauge the extent to which a shareholder would support this end?

For corporations with numerous and diffuse shareholders, few of whom are personally known to management, it is implausible that managers could know the sentiments of all shareholders towards other stakeholders where specific cases may arise concerning the well-being of the latter. If the extent to which a 'duty of beneficence' is binding depends upon personal sensibilities and the degree to which individual needs are fulfilled, then even if management *did* have knowledge of the ethical position of each shareholder, they would be unlikely to secure unanimous agreement on how to act. This situation may well arise because of a lack of consensus among shareholders as to the relative exigency of various stakeholder demands upon the corporation's resources. If a presumption of uniformity among the goals of shareholders (where these deviate from financial gain) is in most cases unwarranted, then it can be asked whether any ethical or legal basis exists for managerial action that does *not* aim primarily at the augmentation of shareholder wealth.

Prior to considering a solution to this difficulty, an example of the problem can be seen in the argument of the Tax Justice Network (TJN) against corporate tax avoidance. In 2005, the TJN estimated that governments were losing up to US$255 billion worldwide each year because of low taxation of funds in offshore centres and tax havens (2005: 3). This is argued to have destructive effects on the development of poor countries and leads to indefensible inequalities between rich and poor (ibid.). They criticise the consequences that follow from tax avoidance: 'the victims of this predatory culture are the poorest and most vulnerable people on the planet' (2005: 7) and

'Unjust tax practices incur costs which fall most heavily on poor people' (2005: 21). What makes the position of the TJN relevant here is that they acknowledge the shareholder perspective that managers have a contractual duty to maximise profits within the law (2005: 19, 34). However, they surmise that if the majority of shareholders were asked to consent to legal tax avoidance, they would in fact decline to maximise their financial wealth at the expense of their tax payments.

The TJN contend that most shareholders wish to pay taxes out of a desire to advance social goals such as providing sufficient revenue 'to fund the physical and social infrastructure essential to economic welfare, and also to enable a degree of wealth distribution between rich and poor' (2005: 11). They state: 'tax minimisation does not necessarily reflect the views of real shareholders' partly because 'tax provides health, education, welfare, the maintenance of peace and stability and other benefits on which communities depend' (2005: 20). Furthermore, they conjecture that 'investors might want to invest in companies that are managed on an ethical basis. Many aggressive tax avoidance practices would be considered ethically unacceptable' (ibid.).

The critical point here is the uncertainty of the suppositions the argument relies upon. Writing of the views of 'real' shareholders, the TJN use phrases such as 'investors might want' (2005: 20), 'it is fair to assume' (2005: 35), and tax minimisation is 'not necessarily' favoured by all shareholders (2005: 19). Such statements suggest a lack of specificity and the difficulty of envisaging the ends that actual shareholders would adopt if confronted with the relevant ethical circumstances. Besides refraining from taking advantage of opportunities for tax avoidance, such circumstances might include the question of whether to pay a living wage to workers in developing countries where a legally enforced minimum is not in place, or whether to invest in new technology that is more environmentally sustainable but also costlier than the alternatives.

Does this ambiguity present a convincing reason for managers *not* to pursue the well-being of non-shareholding stakeholders? Certainly, such a view is consistent with the conclusions of Friedman and other shareholder theorists. It can be argued that managers and shareholders who wish to invest philanthropically should do so with money not invested for business purposes. On the other hand, it is undeniable that many corporations have the resources to invest in the well-being of various stakeholders without seriously impairing their own competitiveness in the market. It has to be remembered that Kant's 'duties of virtue' towards others are 'wide' and 'imperfect' obligations. Only the 'supreme principle' of virtue, from which the duties are derived, is categorically binding: 'act in accordance with a maxim of *ends* that it can be a universal law for everyone to have' (1797/1996: 157). If this principle is ruled out altogether in the use of the corporation's property, then not only would there be no application of the principle to specific cases, but there would be no adherence to this part of ethics at all. Kant's moral system shows the consistency of holding that moral agents are subject both to 'duties of right' *and* to 'duties of virtue' (including a 'duty of beneficence' to make the happiness of others one's end). To restrict the moral use of corporate property merely to what can be justified by property and contract rights, as Friedman and Sternberg do, is therefore mistaken.

Ethical discretion in company law

I now examine the extent to which flexibility exists in UK company law for managers to act on 'imperfect' duties towards stakeholders. Specifically, it can be asked what scope managers have to exercise discretion in how they choose to invest the assets of a business to take into account the ethical concerns of stakeholders affected by business activities, without being held accountable to shareholders for a breach of contractual duty.

This section engages briefly with recent changes in UK company law, particularly with the Companies Act 2006 (which came into force fully in 2009), in which greater latitude appears to exist for ethical discretion on the part of managers, without their being held to have breached a fiduciary duty to shareholders. The focus here is on the United Kingdom for no other reason than the present author's familiarity with it; however, there is a clear similarity between this analysis and Lea's (2004) discussion of 'other constituencies legislation' in the United States. Referring to the passing of company laws in certain jurisdictions in the United States, Lea writes:

The statutes authorise decisions done in the interests of non-shareholder stakeholders but do not prescribe, specify or require any particular form of behaviour to be done in the interests of these stakeholders... in effect,

the law is recognising the open ended nature of these obligations and legit-
imising decisions that are done on that basis while, at the same time, recognising that one cannot enforce or constrain a defined pattern of behaviour.
(2004: 210)

Lea (2004) argues that such legislation permits managers to act on
imperfect duties towards a company's stakeholders.

Before looking at the latest UK Companies Act, it should be noted
that a few years ago the Community Interest (Audit, Investigations and
Community Enterprise) Act 2004 was passed. This Act 'provides for a
new type of company to be known as a community interest company
(CIC). This is for social enterprises who want to use their profits and
assets for the benefit of the public' (Dine and Koutsias 2007: 19). This
might be taken as an example of a type of organisation in which management would have greater ethical discretion in spending shareholder
wealth. However, as with a for-profit business, management would still
have responsibility for acting in accordance with the constitution of
the firm, and would be held accountable by shareholders for fulfilling
their contractual obligations in this regard. They would not necessarily
have any more flexibility in deviating from this contract, or interpreting it in the light of their own ethical perception, in circumstances not
covered by the company's objects in its memorandum of association.

According to Dine and Koutsias (2007), a company's memorandum
of association was considered before 2006 to be its most important
document. It included within it the objects of a company from which
the directors could not deviate. However, from the Companies Act
2006 (section 31): 'Unless a company's articles specifically restrict the
objects of the company, its objects are unrestricted' and according to
section 39: 'The validity of an act done by a company shall not be called
into question on the ground of lack of capacity by reason of anything
in the company's constitution' (Dine and Koutsias 2007: 46). These
sections imply that if management is largely unrestricted by a statement
of objects, then in situations in which a 'duty of virtue' may clash with
a contractual duty to shareholders, there is greater legal scope for an
ethical interpretation of shareholder interests. Furthermore, according
to the new law, if the actions of directors are considered to be outside
the scope of the company's constitution, then it is up to shareholders
to bring an injunction voluntarily against the directors. This is not

something that can be imposed on the firm from outside (ibid.). Again, the implication is a greater potential alignment between the ethical discretion of management and the actual ethical values of shareholders, even if these are unknown to management at the time that an ethical decision has to be made.

An implication of this change concerns the rights of outside parties contracting with the corporation. Rather than a contract with a party being void if management act outside the objects in the company's memorandum, it is instead assumed that *any* contract entered into with a person acting in good faith is binding. Section 40 of the Companies Act (2006) reads: 'In favour of a person dealing with a company in good faith, the power of the directors to bind the company, or authorise others to do so, is deemed to be free of any limitation under the company's constitution' (cited in Dine and Koutsias 2007: 49). Dine and Koutsias (2007: 49) summarise the effect of this provision of the new Act: 'once an act has been done by a company, that act can only very rarely be challenged on the *ultra vires* basis so as to upset the rights of third parties'. As the legal rights of third parties are likely to be affected by an ethical decision to use corporate assets to pursue stakeholder ends, a change in the law that protects the rights of third parties may have the effect of widening the scope for ethical discretion on the part of management.

Another recent change to the law concerns the ability of shareholders to ratify acts of directors which are allegedly *ultra vires* (exceeding their powers). Under the 1985 Act a special resolution, requiring a 75% majority, had to be passed by shareholders to ratify acts that fall outside the constitution of the company. However, under the Companies Act 2006, this requirement has been reduced to an *ordinary* resolution requiring only a simple majority (Dine and Koutsias 2007: 50). A possible effect of this change would again be greater managerial freedom in anticipating the ethical objectives that shareholders might wish to adopt. If there are circumstances in which the ethical choice a shareholder might make lies beyond the scope of the company's constitution, this change would give management more scope for taking this into account. Indeed, under the old case law, it was consistently held that even *with* the express consent of all shareholders, the company could not be bound by any actions it took outside the powers given to it by the memorandum (Dine and Koutsias 2007: 50–1). The new law would seem to permit greater freedom to pursue the subjective interests of shareholders even where these are not reducible to the objects of the company.

The changes brought about by the Companies Act 2006 can of course be analysed in much greater detail. The simple observation made here is that the weakening of the restrictions previously imposed on a company by a statement of 'objects' (and the lessening of the importance of the memorandum itself) can have the effect of increasing the scope for the ethical discretion that management can exercise on behalf of shareholders. The problem with the shareholder theory, even in its deontological version, is that it fails to conceptualise the variability of ends sought by the principals to whom management is accountable. Even if there is no necessary uniformity in the way that a 'duty of virtue' is apparent to any individual, and the same difficulty with formalising the duties of shareholders in a statement of objects would be found in responding to the purposes of a number of diverse shareholders, the changes to the law suggest that management is no longer restricted to those actions that *can* be uniformly stated.

Of course, there is the question of the basis that remains for holding management accountable in the absence of a binding statement of objects. However, the relevant point about 'duties of virtue' is that they cannot be reduced to a set of principles that apply equally to all. Therefore, the ethical perspective of a corporation as represented by management, who act (according to the shareholder theory) as agents for the shareholders, is incomplete without a space for the pursuit of ethical objectives that cannot be formally stated. The recent legislative changes suggest that it is now possible, at least to a greater extent than before, for this fact to be accommodated in the decision making of managers within the rule of law.

Conclusion

The aim of this chapter has been to place my argument that a corporation should be run in the interest of its shareholders in the context of other theories that have led to the same conclusion. It was also to explore the practical limitations of these arguments. It was found that two separate critiques of stakeholder theory in favour of profit maximisation have been developed, both of which are responses to the problem caused by the separation of ownership and control in the modern corporation. Jensen (2002) and others reject on consequentialist grounds any solution offered by stakeholder theory or CSR. A lack of accountability with a risk of managerial opportunism is argued to be a damaging effect of replacing the single objective of profit maximisation with a stakeholder governance model.

However, a coherent response from Sacconi (2004) and others is that management can pursue the single objective of maximising profits prior to the distribution of these profits in accordance with notions of fairness or distributive justice. In theory this points to the inadequacy of profit maximisation and accountability as moral criteria for an alternative to stakeholder theory. The deontological shareholder theory, on the other hand, is based on moral constraints that are not contingent on the consequences that would occur from their observation in practice. This version is consistent with arguments developed earlier in the book, in which ethical principles intrinsic to a market economy exist as constraints on the pursuit of any corporate objective.

The internal limitations of this rights-based contractual theory were then explored. It was argued that the ethical perspective of a corporation should not be limited to the observation by management of a contractual ('perfect') duty to act in the formal interests of shareholders. Instead there should be latitude for responding, perhaps only as a temporary deviation from financial gain, to the needs of stakeholders in situations that are not covered by a formal statement of objects, or by traditional performance objectives such as profit maximisation. This ethical discretion is still perfectly consistent with the shareholder theory of the firm, as the ends of shareholders and not those of any other group are still the determining factor. However, what is missing from current versions of shareholder theory is a conceptualisation of the breadth of these interests (beyond financial gain), which I have tried to illustrate through Kant's distinction between 'duties of virtue' and 'duties of right'. Turning to the Companies Act of 2006, which came fully into force in 2009, it can be seen that greater flexibility now exists in UK law for management to act on a broader range of shareholder interests.

7 | Conclusion

This book began by showing the importance of stakeholder theory in the context of two radically opposed viewpoints on the social responsibility of the corporation. In response to growing public concern, many have argued that the fundamental flaw of the modern corporation is its mandate to pursue shareholder value relentlessly and without concern for ethical standards. As long as the business corporation is accountable to its shareholders alone, it remains unsustainable as a social institution. Perhaps the best-known version of this view is found in Bakan's (2004) *The Corporation*. Against this position it is argued by Milton Friedman (1970) and libertarian defenders of the free market that for the corporation to pursue an objective that is *not* reducible to shareholder interests is ethically unacceptable. Stakeholder theory is potentially significant in that it seeks to avoid these polarised views.

Stakeholder theory therefore appeals to those who are concerned with the ethical responsibilities of the corporation but are not inclined towards the extremes of an anti-corporate or libertarian perspective. Its influence on the mindset of corporate executives is illustrated by Agle and Agle (2007), who found that on the websites of 100 companies drawn from the Fortune 500, 64 embraced approaches to 'maximise the well-being of stakeholders' while only 10 advocated the 'pure stockholder' approach of maximising value for shareholders (cited in Agle and Mitchell 2008: 153–4). This development in the outlook of corporations may reflect a move toward a stakeholder perspective in the customers, investors, employees and other stakeholders on whom a corporation depends. Furthermore, this may also be the case with corporate legislation. Campbell and Kitson (2008) observe that the proposal for an operating and financial review legally requiring directors in the United Kingdom to 'provide an account of the company's key relationships with employees, customers, suppliers and others on which its success depends' (Department for Trade and Industry 2000, cited in Campbell and Kitson 2008: 18) was heavily influenced by stakeholder theory.

As a normative idea, this theory clearly has the potential to shape to a significant extent what is expected of the business corporation in society, and evidence suggests it is already doing so. What I have argued is that there is a crucial problem at the heart of the theory which, if irresolvable, means the theory is gravely misconceived. An attempt to act or legislate on the basis of its principles will therefore lead to outcomes that none of its protagonists intend. In the case of the two competing perspectives with which the book began, it was seen that despite their opposed perspectives on the ethical viability of the corporation, they share the assumption that the only corporate objective consistent with the context of a market economy is the pursuit of shareholder wealth. Capitalism and the shareholder perspective are seen as necessarily connected. In contrast, the crucial argument made by stakeholder theorists is that one can embrace the market economy while abandoning the shareholder perspective. The aim of this book has been to examine this central claim.

In other words, the aim is to test whether any version of stakeholder theory is possible in a market economy. To answer this question logically required two pieces of information: (1) the normative arguments of stakeholder theory and (2) the ethical principles of a market economy. The first part was covered in Chapters 2 and 3. Chapter 2 engaged with the history and scope of the stakeholder idea, looking at the etymology of the concept and some of the uses to which it has been put in organisation theory. Besides an 'instrumental' or 'strategic' branch of the concept, four distinct normative arguments were identified. One involved the idea of a 'social contract' to represent an association between all the stakeholders of a firm, another invoked the 'public interest' as the basis of corporate responsibility, a third appealed to the idea of 'distributive justice' as a criterion for adjudicating between stakeholder claims, and a fourth relied on the 'principle of fairness'. Chapter 3 then explored the philosophical concepts underpinning these arguments. The first three arguments are premised on an idea of the corporation as a contractually created association of all its stakeholders, each of whom delegates power to an executive (management) whose function is to realise the common purpose for which the association is created. The fourth (the 'principle of fairness') makes no such assumption, and concerns merely the relationship of an individual to an organisation rather than the basis of the organisation itself.

The second question was answered in the first half of Chapter 4. A minimal set of elements that can be seen as belonging to the concept of market exchange or trade were expounded, and it was asked what ethical principles would have to be observed if a simple act of trade is morally permissible. Without the observation of a minimum of two principles – a right to property and a right of contract – trade itself would have no ethical status. A market economy, based essentially on trade, is therefore inconceivable without these principles and a logical requirement of stakeholder theory is that it conforms to them.

With these two pieces of information in place, an analysis of the consistency of stakeholder theory with a market economy could then be carried out. The second half of Chapter 4 engaged with this problem in the context of the last of the four arguments discussed earlier. As the 'principle of fairness' makes no assumption about an association of all stakeholders whose interests are represented by the corporation, it was valid to apply the principles of a market economy to the corporation considered simply as a commercial organisation. In other words, the relationship between a corporation and its stakeholders was conceived as being based not on representation but on *exchange*. When the principles of contract and property were applied to the corporation understood in this way, it was found that the corporate objective reduces to a representation of shareholder interests, and cannot include the interests of any other stakeholders.

Chapter 5 continued the analysis by turning to the assumption at the basis of the other normative arguments. The previous chapter adduced legal and historical evidence for a view of the corporation as a commercial entity, to which the relevant ethical principles were then applied. The problem in Chapter 4 was to see if an application of these principles to this concept of the corporation could yield a version of stakeholder theory. However, Chapter 5 asks whether the view of the corporation assumed by the other three types of normative argument is in the first place justifiable. If this concept of the corporation cannot be supported, then any normative conclusions that follow from it cannot be justified. The question is whether a corporation can be seen as a broad association of the interests of *all* its stakeholders, with the corporate objective a representation of this collective interest. For a variety of reasons, it was argued that no such collective interest exists, and the view of the corporation described in the previous chapter is the correct one. This being the case, no valid conclusions about the ethical purposes of the corporation can be drawn from *any* of the first three categories of argument elucidated in Chapter 2. Only the 'principle of fairness' is compatible with a correct concept of the corporation. However, when analysed in the light of property and contract rights, only the shareholder theory of the firm can be sustained.

If most stakeholder theorists have assumed (implicitly or explicitly) an empirical view of the corporation that is demonstrably false, and a view for which there is greater evidence can support only the shareholder theory, it appears that the two normative commitments which underpin the stakeholder idea and are responsible for its great appeal are ultimately irreconcilable. The ethical framework of a market economy cannot permit a corporate objective that embodies the interests of any stakeholder group other than the shareholders.

However, this abstract conclusion does not address the institutional problem of how mechanisms of accountability and governance could be designed within the field of possibilities available under this conclusion. It may be that the very basic principles elaborated in Chapter 4 leave a degree of freedom for other (non-contradictory) principles that are abstractions from other aspects of ethical experience. It is this question that was addressed in Chapter 6. After a survey of some of the best-known critiques of CSR and arguments for the shareholder theory, a distinction between 'perfect' and 'imperfect' duties in the work of Kant (1797/1996) was used to elucidate a principle that is relevant for the corporate objective, and consistent with the principles of a market economy, without being logically entailed by them. Indeed, while remaining consistent with the abstract principles of the market, a corporation can be structured through legal, cultural and institutional mechanisms to foster other moral principles to a greater or lesser extent. It was speculated that the difficulty of reconciling what Kant calls 'duties of virtue' (e.g., a benevolent duty to pursue the happiness of others) with the diversity of ownership in modern large corporations and the ethical 'distance' of managers from the sensibilities of individual shareholders, may lie at the root of many of the moral complaints and grievances levelled at corporations. However, it was held that various changes in the UK Companies Act of 2006 offer the flexibility for managers to act in accordance with these 'duties of

virtue' and without deviation from the framework of a market economy. A fuller analysis of the way in which mechanisms of law and corporate governance can foster different kinds of virtue in organisations
is unfortunately beyond the scope of this book, although much research
has already been carried out in this area.[1]

With this analysis, it can be concluded that stakeholder theory advocates a set of ethical positions which, though having intuitive appeal
when considered independently, turn out upon inspection to be inconsistent with each other. However, it can be asked *why* stakeholder
theorists are inclined to conflate these different ethical positions. Is
there perhaps an identification of two separate entities with similar
qualities, but crucial differences that are overlooked? In the case of
the first three normative arguments, the question is why the economic
relationship of a corporation with its stakeholders is considered as if
it had the qualities of a state. In this concluding chapter I will offer
a few reflections on the problem. This may help to highlight both the
reasons for the appeal of stakeholder theory and the nature of the
contradiction which lies at the heart of it.

In asking what abstract qualities can be attributed to a state and
how they compare to those of a market economy comprising corporate
stakeholders, it is first necessary to note the breadth of interpretations
of the state through history. According to Michael Oakeshott (2006),
in his *Lectures in the History of Political Thought*,[2] writers such as
Hobbes, Locke and Rousseau see the bonds that tie together the citizens
of a state as the work of human artifice. A state is not understood as
the work of God and/or something 'natural' to be subscribed to out of
'necessity', but a creation of human beings with a deliberate purpose.

Oakeshott argues that this understanding of the state as an *artificial* association reflects a change in human sentiment characteristic of
modern Europe: 'the belief that each individual human being was a
'natural' unity and had no natural ties with any other human being'
(2006: 415). He argues that the context of this idea was the dissolution
of those communal ties and feudal relationships which composed the
structure of life in medieval communities (2006: 416). Tenancies of

---

[1] See Solomon (1999: 30–7) for a good introduction. For a critique of this
research see Jones et al. (2005: 56–68).

[2] This work comprises previously unpublished lectures given by Oakeshott at
the London School of Economics and Political Science during the late 1960s,
shortly before he retired as Professor of Political Science.

land came to be seen in terms of contracts for money rents, and the guild organisation of industry gave way to 'individual enterprise and partnerships springing from individual choice' (ibid.). For these reasons, Oakeshott writes that the modern state 'generated the unattached individual . . . [T]he separate, individual man, with no apparent "natural" ties, was appearing on the scene' (ibid.). However, this particular interpretation of the state as a product of human artifice (to which the 'social contract' tradition belongs), can be contrasted with at least two other perspectives in which a state arises through very different means. Oakeshott notes an intellectual disposition at the time of the emergence of the modern state: 'On one side, there was the "natural" world, understood in Christian thought as the work of God; on the other side, there were the works of men, the world of "artifice"' (2006: 413), a common view in Western Europe from classical antiquity until the eighteenth century. Accordingly, any kind of association *not* considered to be a work of art created for a specifically human purpose must to some extent be part of the natural world of 'necessity' and beyond alteration by human choice.

In the political experience of modern Europe, there was apparently a strong motive for finding something more than a merely artificial bond for the members of a state. In Oakeshott's view, the modern state 'emerged in violence, in the imposition of territorial boundaries which cut across "natural" communities, which severed "natural" ties, and which destroyed ancient allegiances' (2006: 415). While on the one hand this situation could be taken to suggest that the state is not a 'natural' community of any kind, it is also conceivable that the loss of the familiarity of the local community created a vacuum in which 'a search for a "natural" unity for a "state", something to correspond with the lost "natural" (blood) unity of a "tribe" or a "people", is not difficult to account for' (2006: 411). If this historical interpretation is accurate, it gives an explanation for the emergence of theories conceiving of the state as an 'organic unity', an organism, or 'a natural whole of functionally related parts' (2006: 405). According to Oakeshott, under this broad conception of the state as a 'natural' association, some writers liken it to the human body, with the role of government being that of the brain in controlling the parts of the body; some liken it to the communities of the 'social insects' such as ants and bees; and others (e.g., Jean Bodin and Robert Filmer) compare it to the patriarchal family or household. Finally, drawing on the Latin word *natio*,[3] the familiar concept of 'nationality' has emerged to describe the bond that ties together members of a state (Oakeshott 2006: 405–10).

If this is one way in which the 'state' can be understood *other* than as an artificial creation serving a specific purpose, then another understanding presents it as a hybrid of 'nature' and 'artifice', namely as something *historical*. If it is assumed that what is natural is necessary and cannot be other than it is, but 'the world of "history" is the world of things which are contingent, and might have been other than they are' (2006: 421), then to describe something as 'historical' is to describe it as lying at least partly outside the world of nature and necessity. However, if a genuine artefact is made to serve a specific premeditated purpose, whereas what is 'historical' is partly the product of time and circumstance, then to describe the state as a 'historical' entity is describe it as neither entirely natural nor artificial (ibid.). Oakeshott (2006: 423) holds that this view is best seen in the writings of Edmund Burke, a view in which

a 'state' is to be understood as a collection of human beings who have no 'natural' ties, who are not united by common blood, who cannot be supposed to have entered into an express agreement to associate with one another for the achievement of a specific purpose, but whom chance has brought together, and who have acquired a sentiment of solidarity from having enjoyed, over the years, a common and continuous 'historical' experience. (2006: 421–2)

Given the existence of these other interpretations of what constitutes a 'state', it is clear that rather than looking at the features of states generally, it is a very *specific* theory of the state as an 'artificial' association that is relevant to stakeholder theory. What stakeholder theorists have assumed is that this understanding of the state is a good enough analogy for the relationships a corporation enjoys with its stakeholders for it to serve as a premise in reaching conclusions about the ethical objectives of the corporation. It has been argued that in decisive respects the analogy does not hold. However, it is still worth reflecting upon

---

[3] Oakeshott (2006: 407–8) writes: 'The Latin word *natio* was originally understood for a group of human beings, larger than a family but smaller than a "people" (*populus*), which was distinguished from other groups in respect of . . . a language of their own, perhaps the presumption of common blood, and an exclusive religion'.

the features these two forms of association have in common, as well as the implications of conflating the two and thereby overlooking the crucial differences between them.

Perhaps the most obvious feature that both types of association have in common is their inter-subjective nature. If an organisation's stakeholders are classified as those without whose support the organisation would cease to exist (using the definition of the Stanford Research Institute) then a necessary condition for the accrual of benefits to any individual stakeholder is the participation of all other stakeholders. Likewise, in the concept of the state as an artificial association, the consent of all subjects in submitting to a sovereign authority is a universal condition for the legitimate enjoyment of the protection offered by that sovereign. In this sense the mutual dependence of each corporate stakeholder on every other, and of each citizen of a state on every other, is a point of commonality in the two types of association.

It can also be observed that the engagement of the members of each type of association is voluntary and aimed at the satisfaction of individual needs. There is no assumption amongst stakeholder theorists or philosophers of the social contract that the motive for forming an association is a benevolent desire to contribute to a common good. Just as individuals entering into exchange relationships with the corporation can do so to satisfy separate ends, the members of a state entering a 'social contract' are not assumed to have a common purpose other than the protection of their individual rights or the preservation of their lives. Both sorts of arrangement appear to encompass the choice of free individuals in satisfying their personal desires.[4]

---

[4] However, it should be noted that for many writers, particularly those in a Marxist tradition, this comparison would be tenuous. Inasmuch as stakeholders bargain with a corporation in acts of market exchange, the 'freedom' of the separate contractors can be considered a question-begging assumption. Marx, in Volume One of *Capital*, writes: 'In the market, as owner of the commodity "labour-power", [our worker] stood face to face with other owners of commodities, one owner against another owner. The contract by which he sold his labour-power to the capitalist proved in black and white, so to speak, that he was free to dispose of himself. But when the transaction was concluded, it was discovered that he was no "free agent", that the period of time for which he is free to sell his labour-power is the period of time for which he is forced to sell it' (1867/1976: 415–16). See also the discussion about exploitation and 'formal freedom' in Alex Callinicos's (2003: 36, 115) *An Anti-Capitalist Manifesto*.

In acting for the satisfaction of their personal objectives in an arrangement of mutual dependence on one another, corporate stakeholders and the citizens of a state benefit from a certain *order* in their affairs. In both arrangements, the confidence with which each individual can expect the actions of others to correspond to what is necessary for the satisfaction of their ends is an advantage of entering such an arrangement. In Chapter 4 it was argued that the stability of a market economy depends upon the protection of rights to property and contractual fulfilment, and if these rights are guaranteed then market exchange can flourish as a rational activity. As shown in Chapter 3, the theorists of the social contract contend that individuals in a 'State of Nature' would be rational to submit to a sovereign authority with the power to enforce order and secure the life, liberty and possessions of their citizens. Both types of association in question can be considered *ordered* arrangements. The general importance of this idea is elucidated by F. A. Hayek (1982) in the first volume of his *Law, Legislation and Liberty*:

Living as members of society and dependent for the satisfaction of most of our needs on various forms of co-operation with others, we depend for the effective pursuit of our aims clearly on the correspondence of the expectations concerning the actions of others on which our plans are based with what they will really do. This matching of the intentions and expectations that determine the actions of different individuals is the form in which order manifests itself in social life. (1982, I: 36)

In addition to being ordered arrangements in which individuals choose to interact for mutual benefit, another important respect in which the two arrangements are similar is the formal moral equality of the participants. Chapter 4 held that moral rights concerning property and contracts are applicable equally to all if trade is to be considered a rational activity from the perspective of any participant in market exchange. Likewise, it was seen in Chapter 3 that it is one of the duties of the holder of sovereign power to ensure the equality of all subjects before the rule of law. Legislation should be based on abstract principles that do not refer to the particular circumstances of identifiable individuals.

In all these ways a similarity can be seen between a corporation's network of stakeholders and the collection of people who compose the artificial association of a 'state', according to the strand of political philosophy drawn upon by stakeholder theorists. It is conceivable for these reasons that stakeholder theorists have used an (often implicit) analogy between these two forms of association as a basis for their normative conclusions. However, differences exist which make this analogy unsustainable. The relationships formed between a corporation and its stakeholders must be seen to embody *different* subjective values as a necessary criterion for trade. There can be no common purpose binding together the stakeholders of a corporation in the same way that the members of a state can be assumed to consent (if they are rational) to the law of a sovereign power. As Hayek (1982) argues, the act of barter or exchange is a key factor in enabling persons with otherwise conflicting purposes to enter into peaceful collaboration with one another. He writes:

The parties are in fact the more likely to benefit from exchange the more their needs differ... So long as collaboration presupposes common purposes, people with different aims are necessarily enemies who may fight each other for the same means; only the introduction of barter made it possible for the different individuals to be of use to each other without agreeing on the ultimate ends. (1982, II: 109–10)

It was also argued in Chapter 5 that whereas a sovereign is chosen with the consent of his or her subjects to act as a representative for their interests, amongst the stakeholders of a corporation no such representative emerges in pursuit of a common purpose.

However, it could be argued to the contrary that if economic agents are considered both as rational and (as participants in market exchange) as having an equal interest in protecting specific rights, then there would be a common interest in consenting to establish a power for the joint protection of their rights. As Campbell and Kitson argue:

It is true that, in a perfectly competitive market, free riders can benefit from dishonesty and honest traders will be disadvantaged by it. This process can continue until the supply of honest traders runs out and the market it totally corrupted... Thus, a perfectly competitive market must be maintained by legal and/or social regulation that imposes on all those obligations that honest traders impose on themselves. It is, therefore, in the interest of those who do not need to be regulated that they be regulated. (2008: 8)

A similar argument is made by Hayek in relation to the enforcement of the rules necessary for the functioning of a market economy:

Although it is conceivable that the spontaneous order which we call society may exist without government, if the minimum of rules required for the formation of such an order is observed without an organized apparatus for their enforcement, in most circumstances the organization which we call government becomes indispensable in order to assure that those rules are obeyed. (1982, I: 47)

This argument resonates with Scherer and Palazzo's (2011) view that if governments are unable to provide effective regulation of the market, then corporations may have a democratic responsibility to provide it themselves. While these authors do not make the argument directly, what they present may be evidence for a common interest among a corporation's stakeholders, in the light of which stakeholders can be considered an association united by a common purpose. However, while it may be rational for participants in any market economy to consent to the imposition of certain rules of conduct to protect their rights, the claim here is that a corporation's management cannot be the representative of any such purpose. As the overall issue under consideration is the choice of a corporation's objective, it must be kept in mind that a corporation's stakeholders (with the exception of government, if this is counted as a stakeholder) are only related to the corporation through circumstantial economic transactions, and the individuals and companies that are at one moment 'stakeholders' may no longer be so as circumstances change. There is no basis for arguing that corporations represent a general interest of all their stakeholders in securing the minimal rights necessary for a market economy when the existence of any relationship between a corporation and its stakeholders is contingent on a variety of changing circumstances. Furthermore, as pointed out earlier, the existence of the corporation as a legal person implies the existence of a legal system and, in most cases, a sovereign power that enforces the necessary rules of conduct for the market.[5] If these assumptions are made, as they are by most stakeholder theorists, then the corporation cannot have this role.

[5] Scherer and Palazzo (2011) rightly claim that different normative questions emerge if this is not the case. However, to establish the extent to which this *is* the context in which corporations operate requires a separate empirical argument. Crane et al. (2008: 61) point to some relevant considerations.

If the business corporation is not considered in relation to its stakeholders to be merely a part of the market, but instead the representative of a common interest, this can only have the effect of seriously impairing the operation of the market wherever business corporations are involved. Through making the unfounded assumption that a network of individuals or organisations cooperating for mutual advantage must be guided by a common purpose, a mechanism through which a *diversity* of values and purposes co-exist for mutual benefit is compromised in a fundamental way. If the assumptions of stakeholder theory are consistently put into practice one would see a centralisation and monopolisation of economic decision-making power in the hands of corporate managers, with all the divergent interests that a variety of stakeholders might currently pursue (e.g., an employee accepting a cut in pay for greater job satisfaction, or a customer choosing to pay an increase in price for a 'fair trade' product) submerged into a single interest or group of interests which management must represent.

It has been argued that the voluntary consent of all stakeholders (however these are defined) to such a common purpose cannot be assumed. Such an assumption would violate the basic rights that all stakeholders possess as individuals in a society in which cooperation through market exchange is accepted. For this reason, none of the normative arguments for stakeholder theory are consistent with the ethical framework of a market economy, or indeed with capitalism itself. As long as the basic institution of the market and the values that underpin it continue to play a role in our societies, then the ultimate objective of the business corporation cannot be distinguished from that of its nominal owners, the shareholders. Questions should be asked as to whether shareholder theory has its limitations in corporations with large diversified shareholdings, and whether recent developments in corporate law might help to facilitate a more acceptable version of this approach. It can be concluded, however, that within the ethical structure of a market economy the only objective that a corporation can pursue will be that which is consistent with the interests of shareholders.

References

Agle, B. and Agle, L. 2007. The stated objectives of the Fortune 500: Examining the philosophical approaches that drive America's largest firms. Unpublished Working Paper, University of Pittsburgh

Agle, B. and Mitchell, R. 2008. Introduction: Recent research and new questions, in Agle, B., Donaldson, T., Freeman, R., Jensen, M., Mitchell, R., and Wood, D. (eds.) Dialogue: Toward superior stakeholder theory, *Business Ethics Quarterly* 18(2): 153–90

Alborn, T. 1998. *Conceiving Companies: Joint-Stock Politics in Victorian England*. London, Routledge

Alchian, A. and Demsetz, H. 1972. Production, information costs, and economic organization, *American Economic Review* 61(2): 380–7

Bainbridge, S. 1993. In defense of the shareholder wealth maximization norm: A reply to Professor Green, *Washington and Lee Law Review* 50(3): 1423–48

Bakan, J. 2004. *The Corporation: The Pathological Pursuit of Profit and Power*. London, Constable

Becker, L. 1977. *Property Rights: Philosophic Foundations*. Boston, Routledge and Kegan Paul

Becker, L. 1992. Places for pluralism, *Ethics* 102(4): 707–19

Berle, A. and Means, G. 1932. *The Modern Corporation and Private Property*. New York, Macmillan

Blair, M. 1995. *Ownership and Control: Rethinking Corporate Governance for the Twenty-First Century*. Washington, DC, The Brookings Institution

Blair, T. 1996. The Singapore speech, 7 January 1996

Boatright, J. 1994. Fiduciary duties and the shareholder–management relation: Or, what's so special about shareholders? *Business Ethics Quarterly* 4(4): 393–407

Bowen, H. 1953. *Social Responsibilities of the Businessman*. New York, Harper and Brothers

Bowie, N. 2012. Stakeholder theory: The state of the art, in Book Reviews, *Business Ethics Quarterly* 22(1): 179–98

British Broadcasting Corporation 2006. Today, British Broadcasting Corporation (broadcast on BBC Radio 4 on Thursday 5 January 2006)

Burton, B. and Dunn, C. 1996. Feminist ethics as moral grounding for stakeholder theory, *Business Ethics Quarterly* 6(2): 133–47

Callinicos, A. 2003. *An Anti-Capitalist Manifesto*. Cambridge, Polity Press

Campbell, R. and Kitson, A. 2008. *The Ethical Organisation*. 2nd edn. Hampshire, Palgrave Macmillan

Carroll, A. 1999. Corporate social responsibility: Evolution of a definitional construct, *Business and Society* 38(3): 268–95

Child, J. and Marcoux, A. 1999. Freeman and Evan: Stakeholder theory in the original position, *Business Ethics Quarterly* (9)2: 207–23

Clarke, R. and McGuinness, T. 1987. Introduction, in Clarke, R. and McGuinness, T. (eds.) *The Economics of the Firm*. Oxford, Blackwell

Coase, R. 1937. The nature of the firm, *Economica* 4(16): 386–405

Commission of the European Communities 2001. *Green Paper 'Promoting a European Framework for Corporate Social Responsibility'*. COM (2001) 366 final, Brussels

Conry, E. 1995. A critique of social contracts for business, *Business Ethics Quarterly* 5(2): 187–212

Corporate Watch 2006. *What's Wrong with Corporate Social Responsibility?* London, Corporate Watch

Cragg, W. 2002. Business ethics and stakeholder theory, *Business Ethics Quarterly* 12(2): 113–42

Crane, A., Matten, D. and Moon, J. 2008. *Corporations and Citizenship*. Cambridge, Cambridge University Press

Cranston, M. 1968. Introduction, in Rousseau, J. and Cranston, M. (trans.) *The Social Contract*. London, Penguin Books, pp. 9–43

Cruver, B. 2003. *Enron: Anatomy of Greed – The Unshredded Truth from an Enron Insider*. London, Arrow Books

Darwall, S. 1998. *Philosophical Ethics: An Historical and Contemporary Introduction*. Boulder, CO, Westview

Dembinski, P. 2009. *Finance: Servant or Deceiver? Financialization at the Crossroads*. Cook, K. (trans.) Basingstoke, Palgrave Macmillan

Department for Trade and Industry 2000. Modern company law review for a competitive economy. Consultation Documents, March and November

Dine, J. and Koutsias, M. 2007. *Company Law*. 6th edn. Basingstoke, Palgrave Macmillan

Donaldson, T. 1982. *Corporations and Morality*. Englewood Cliffs, NJ, Prentice-Hall

Donaldson, T. 1999. Response: Making stakeholder theory whole, *Academy of Management Review* 24(2): 237–41

Donaldson, T. and Dunfee, T. 1994. Toward a unified conception of business ethics: Integrative social contracts theory, *Academy of Management Review* 19(2): 252–84

Donaldson, T. and Dunfee, T. 1995. Integrative social contracts theory: A communitarian conception of economic ethics, *Economics and Philosophy* 11(1): 85–112

Donaldson, T. and Dunfee, T. 1999. *Ties That Bind: A Social Contracts Approach to Business Ethics*. Boston, Harvard Business School Press

Donaldson, T. and Preston, L. 1995. The stakeholder theory of the corporation: Concepts, evidence, and implications, *Academy of Management Review* 20(1): 65–91

Etzioni, A. 1998. A communitarian note on stakeholder theory, *Business Ethics Quarterly* 8(4): 679–91

Evans, F. 1908. Evolution of the English joint stock limited trading company (I), *Columbia Law Review* 8(5): 339–61

Freeman, R. 1984. *Strategic Management: A Stakeholder Approach*. London, Pitman

Freeman, R. 1994. The politics of stakeholder theory: Some future directions, *Business Ethics Quarterly* 4(4): 409–21

Freeman, R. 1999. Response: Divergent stakeholder theory, *Academy of Management Review* 24(2): 233–6

Freeman, R. 2008. Ending the so-called 'Friedman–Freeman' Debate, in Agle, B., Donaldson, T., Freeman, R., Jensen, M., Mitchell, R., and Wood, D. Dialogue: Toward superior stakeholder theory, *Business Ethics Quarterly* 18(2): 153–90

Freeman, R. and Evan, W. 1990. Corporate governance: A stakeholder interpretation, *Journal of Behavioural Economics* 19(4): 337–60

Freeman, R. and Phillips, R. 2002. Stakeholder theory: A libertarian defence, *Business Ethics Quarterly* 12(3): 331–49

Freeman, R., Wicks, A., and Parmar, B. 2004. Stakeholder theory and 'the corporate objective revisited', *Organization Science* 15(3): 364–9

Freeman, R., Harrison, J., and Wicks, A. 2007. *Managing for Stakeholders: Survival, Reputation, and Success*. New Haven and London, Yale University Press

Freeman, R., Harrison, J., Wicks, A., Parmar, B., and de Colle, S. 2010. *Stakeholder Theory: The State of the Art*. Cambridge, Cambridge University Press

Friedman, A. and Miles, S. 2006. *Stakeholders: Theory and Practice*. Oxford, Oxford University Press

Friedman, M. 1962. *Capitalism and Freedom*. Chicago, The University of Chicago Press

Friedman, M. 13 September 1970. The social responsibility of business is to increase its profits. *New York Times Magazine*. Online at: www.colorado.edu/studentgroups/libertarians/issues/friedman-soc-resp-business.html. Accessed 20 August 2012

Garriga, E. and Melé, D. 2004. Corporate social responsibility theories: Mapping the territory, *Journal of Business Ethics* 53: 51–71

Goodpaster, K. 1991. Business ethics and stakeholder analysis, *Business Ethics Quarterly* 1(1): 53–73

Graafland, J., Eiffinger, S. and Smid, H. 2004. Benchmarking of corporate social responsibility: Methodological problems and robustness, *Journal of Business Ethics* 53(1–2): 137–52

Gregor, M. 1996. Translator's note on the text, in Kant, I. and Gregor, M. (trans.) *The Metaphysics of Morals*. Cambridge University Press, pp. xxxii–xxxvi

Hayek, F. 1982. *Law, Legislation and Liberty*. London, Routledge

Hayek, F. 1988. *The Fatal Conceit: The Errors of Socialism*. London, Routledge

Hare, R. 1963. A moral argument, in Rachels, J. (ed.) 1998. *Ethical Theory 1: The Question of Objectivity*. New York, Oxford University Press, pp. 51–7

Harris, J. and Freeman, R. 2008. The impossibility of the separation thesis: A response to Joakim Sandberg, *Business Ethics Quarterly* 18(4): 541–8

Hart, H. 1955. Are there any natural rights? *Philosophical Review* 64(2): 175–91

Henderson, D. 2001. *Misguided Virtue: False Notions of Corporate Social Responsibility*. London, The Institute of Economic Affairs

Heugens, P., van Oosterhout, J. and Kaptein, M. 2006. Foundations and applications for contractualist business ethics, *Journal of Business Ethics* 68(3): 211–28

Hobbes, T. 1651/1996. *Leviathan*. Oxford, Oxford University Press

Hodapp, P. 1990. Can there be a social contract with business? *Journal of Business Ethics* 9(2): 127–31

Honoré, A. 1961. Ownership, in Guest, A. (ed.) *Oxford Essays in Jurisprudence*. Oxford, Clarendon Press, pp. 107–47

Höpfl, H. and Thompson, M. 1979. The history of contract as a motif in political thought, *The American Historical Review* 84(4): 919–44

Höpfl, H. 2008. The Critical Issue of Accountability, in Boje, D. (ed.) *Critical Theory Ethics for Business and Public Administration*. Charlotte, NC, Information Age Publishing

Hunt, B. 1935. The joint-stock company in England, 1800–1825, *Journal of Political Economy* 43(1): 1–33

Hutton, W. 1997. *Stakeholding and Its Critics*. London, IEA Health and Welfare Unit

Jackson, K. 1993. Global distributive justice and the corporate duty to aid, *Journal of Business Ethics* 12(7): 547–51

Jensen, M. 2001. Value maximisation, stakeholder theory, and the corporate objective function. Unpublished Working Paper, Harvard Business School

Jensen, M. 2002. Value maximisation, stakeholder theory, and the corporate objective function, *Business Ethics Quarterly* 12(2): 235–56

Jensen, M. 2008. Non-rational behaviour, value conflicts, stakeholder theory, and firm behaviour, in Agle, B., T. Donaldson, R. Freeman, M. Jensen, R. Mitchell, and D. Wood, Dialogue: Toward superior stakeholder theory, *Business Ethics Quarterly* 18(2): 153–90

Jensen, M. and Meckling W. 1976. Theory of the firm: Managerial behaviour, agency costs and ownership structure, *Journal of Financial Economics* 3(4): 305–60

Jones, C., Parker, M. and ten Bos, R. 2005. *For Business Ethics*. London, Routledge

Jones, P. 1994. *Rights*. Basingstoke, Palgrave

Jones, T. and Wicks, A. 1999. Letter to AMR regarding 'convergent stakeholder theory', *Academy of Management Review* 24(4): 621–3

Kaler, J. 2002. Morality and strategy in stakeholder identification, *Journal of Business Ethics* 39: 91–9

Kaler, J. 2003. Differentiating stakeholder theories, *Journal of Business Ethics* 46(1): 71–83

Kaler, J. 2006. Evaluating stakeholder theory, *Journal of Business Ethics* 69(3): 249–68

Kant, I. 1793/1991. On the common saying: 'This may be true in theory, but it does not apply in practice', in Kant, I. and Reiss, H. (ed.) *Political Writings*. 2nd edn. Cambridge, Cambridge University Press, pp. 61–92

Kant, I. 1797/1996. *The Metaphysics of Morals*. Gregor, M. (trans.) Cambridge, Cambridge University Press

Keeley, M. 1995. Continuing the social contract tradition, *Business Ethics Quarterly* 5(2): 241–56

Laplume, A., Sonpar, K., and Litz, R. 2008 Stakeholder theory: Reviewing a theory that moves us, *Journal of Management* 34(6): 1152–89

Lea, D. 2004. The imperfect nature of corporate responsibilities to stakeholders, *Business Ethics Quarterly* 14(2): 201–17

Locke, J. 1689/1988. *Two Treatises of Government*. Student edn. Cambridge, Cambridge University Press

Long, R. 2006. Realism and abstraction in economics: Aristotle and Mises versus Friedman, *Quarterly Journal of Austrian Economics* 9(3): 3–23

Mackie, J. 1977. The subjectivity of values, in Rachels, J. (ed.) 1998. *Ethical Theory 1: The Question of Objectivity*. New York, Oxford University Press, 58–84

Mansell, S. 2010. Business ethics and the question of objectivity: The concept of moral progress in a dialectical framework, in Muhr, S., Sørensen, B. and Vallentin, S. (eds.) *Ethics and Organizational Practice: Questioning the Moral Foundations of Management*. Cheltenham, Edward Elgar, pp. 101–20

Marcoux, A. 2003. A fiduciary argument against stakeholder theory, *Business Ethics Quarterly* 13(1): 1–24

Marx, K. 1847/1955. *The Poverty of Philosophy*. Quelch, H. (trans.) London, Martin Lawrence

Marx, K. 1867/1976. *Capital: Volume 1*. Fowkes, B. (trans.) London, Penguin Books

Marx, K. 1867/1995. *Capital: A New Abridgement*. McLellan, D. (ed.) Oxford, Oxford University Press

McLean, B. and Elkind, P. 2004. *The Smartest Guys in the Room: The Amazing Rise and Scandalous Fall of Enron*. New York, Penguin Books

McMahon, C. 1995. The political theory of organizations and business ethics, *Philosophy and Public Affairs* 24(4): 292–313

McNulty, M. 1975. A question of managerial legitimacy, *Academy of Management Journal* 18(3): 579–88

Mill, J. 1859/1991. On liberty, in Mill, J. and Gray, J. (ed.) *On Liberty and Other Essays*. Oxford, Oxford University Press, pp. 5–128

Mill, J. 1861/1991. Utilitarianism, in Mill, J. and Gray, J. (ed.) *On Liberty and Other Essays*. Oxford, Oxford University Press, pp. 129–201

Mitchell, A. and Sikka, P. 2005. *Taming the Corporations*. Essex, Association for Accountancy & Business Affairs

Mitchell, R. 1986. Corporate power, legitimacy, and social policy, *Western Political Quarterly* 39(2): 197–212

Mitchell, R., Agle, B. and Wood, D. 1997. Toward a theory of stakeholder identification and salience: Defining the principle of who and what really counts, *Academy of Management Review* 22(4): 853–86

Moir, L. 2001. What do we mean by corporate social responsibility? *Corporate Governance* 1(2): 16–22

Moriarty, J. 2005. On the relevance of political philosophy to business ethics, *Business Ethics Quarterly* 15(3): 455–73

Munzer, S. 1990. *A Theory of Property*. Cambridge, Cambridge University Press

Nagel, T. 1980. Value, in Rachels, J. (ed.) 1998. *Ethical Theory 1: The Question of Objectivity*. New York, Oxford University Press, 109–24

Nozick, R. 1974. *Anarchy, State and Utopia*. Oxford, Blackwell

Oakeshott, M. 2006. *Lectures in the History of Political Thought*. Exeter, Imprint Academic

Online Etymology Dictionary 2001. Online at: www.etymonline.com/index. php?search=stake&searchmode=none. Accessed 8 January 2009

Oxford English Dictionary Online 2000. 2nd edn. Online at: http://0-dictionary.oed.com.serlib0.essex.ac.uk/entrance.dtl. Accessed 8 January 2009

Oxford English Dictionary Online, draft revision 2004. Online at: http://0-dictionary.oed.com.serlib0.essex.ac.uk/cgi/entry/00335018? query_type=word&queryword=stakeholder&first=1&max_to_show= 10&sort_type=alpha&result_place=2&search_id=XWRT-jQOVNQ-3002&hilite=00335018. Accessed 8 January 2009

Parker, M. 2002. *Against Management*. Cambridge, Polity Press

Phillips, R. 1997. Stakeholder theory and a principle of fairness, *Business Ethics Quarterly* 7(1): 51–66

Phillips, R. 2003. *Stakeholder Theory and Organizational Ethics*. San Francisco, Berret-Koehler Publishers, Inc.

Phillips, R. and Margolis, J. 1999. Toward an ethics of organizations, *Business Ethics Quarterly* 9(4): 619–38

Plato. 1994. *Republic*. Waterfield, R. (trans.) Oxford, Oxford University Press

Porter, M. and Kramer, M. 2002. The competitive advantage of corporate philanthropy, *Harvard Business Review* 80(12): 56–69

Public Relations Unit, European Court of Human Rights 2012. *The ECHR in 50 Questions*. Online at: www.echr.coe.int/NR/rdonlyres/ 5C53ADA4-80F8-42CB-B8BD-CBBB781F42C8/0/FAQ_ENG_JANV 2012.pdf. Accessed 20 August 2012

Putterman, L. and Kroszner, R. 1996. The economic nature of the firm: A new introduction, in Putterman, L. and Kroszner, R. (eds.) *The Economic Nature of the Firm: A Reader*. Cambridge and New York, Cambridge University Press, pp. 1–34

Rachels, J. (ed.) 1998. *Ethical Theory 1: The Question of Objectivity*. New York, Oxford University Press

Rawls, J. 1999. *A Theory of Justice*. Revised edn. Oxford, Oxford University Press

Reynolds, M. and Yuthas, K. 2008. Moral discourse and corporate social responsibility reporting, *Journal of Business Ethics* 78(1/2): 47–64

Roberts, J. 2003. The manufacture of corporate social responsibility: Constructing corporate sensibility, *Organization* 10(3): 249–65

Rothbard, M. 1982. *The Ethics of Liberty*. New York, New York University Press

Rousseau, J. 1762/1968. *The Social Contract*. Cranston, M. (trans.) London, Penguin Books

Russell, B. 1935. Science and ethics, in Rachels, J. (ed.) 1998. *Ethical Theory 1: The Question of Objectivity.* New York, Oxford University Press, 19–27

Sacconi, L. 2004. *Corporate Social Responsibility (CSR) as a Model of 'Extended' Corporate Governance. An Explanation Based on the Economic Theories of Social Contract, Reputation and Reciprocal Conformism.* Liuc Papers n. 142, Serie Etica, Diritto edn. Economica 10

Sacconi, L. 2006. A social contract account for CSR as an extended model of corporate governance (I): Rational bargaining and justification, *Journal of Business Ethics* 68(3): 259–81

Scherer, G. and Palazzo, G. 2007. Toward a political conception of corporate responsibility: Business and society seen from a Habermasian perspective, *Academy of Management Review* 32(4): 1096–1120

Scherer, G. and Palazzo, G. 2011. The new political role of business in a globalized world: A review of a new perspective on CSR and its implications for the firm, governance, and democracy, *Journal of Management Studies* 48(4): 899–931

Singer, P. (ed.) 1990. *A Companion to Ethics.* Oxford, Blackwell

Skinner, Q. 1989. The state, in Goodin, R. and Pettit, P. (eds.) 1997. *Contemporary Political Philosophy: An Anthology.* Oxford, Blackwell, pp. 3–26

Skinner, Q. 2009. A genealogy of the modern state, *Proceedings of the British Academy* 162: 325–70

Slinger, G. 1999. *Essays on stakeholding,* PhD dissertation, Department of Applied Economics, University of Cambridge

Smith, A. 1776/1970. *The Wealth of Nations: Books I–III.* London, Penguin Books

Smith, R. 2009. Human rights in international law, in Goodhart, M. (ed.) *Human Rights: Politics and Practice.* New York, Oxford University Press, pp. 26–44

Smith, T. 1999. The efficient norm for corporate law: A neo-traditional interpretation of fiduciary duty, *Michigan Law Review* 98(1): 214–68

Solomon, R. 1999. Business ethics and virtue, in Frederick, R. (ed.) *A Companion to Business Ethics.* Maldon, MA, Blackwell, pp. 30–7

Sternberg, E. 2000. *Just Business: Business Ethics in Action.* 2nd edn. Oxford, Oxford University Press

Sternberg, E. 2004. *Corporate Governance: Accountability in the Marketplace.* London, Institute of Economic Affairs

Stevenson, C. 1963. The nature of ethical disagreement, in Rachels, J. (ed.) 1998. *Ethical Theory 1: The Question of Objectivity.* New York, Oxford University Press, 43–50

Stewart, R., Allen, J., and Cavender, J. 1963 *The Strategic Plan*. Research
    Report 168, Stanford Research Institute, Long Range Planning Service,
    Industrial Economics Division

Strong, N. and Waterson, M. 1987. Principals, agents and information,
    in Clarke, R. and McGuiness, T. (eds.) *The Economics of the Firm*.
    Oxford, Blackwell, pp. 18–41

Sundaram, A. and Inkpen, A. 2004. The corporate objective revisited, *Orga-
    nization Science* 15(3): 350–63

Tax Justice Network 2005. *Tax Us if You Can: The True Story of a Global
    Failure*. London, Tax Justice Network

Tencanti, A., Perrini, F., and Pogutz, S. 2004. New tools to foster corporate
    socially responsible behaviour, *Journal of Business Ethics* 53(1/2): 173–
    90

Toenjes, R. 2002. Why be moral in business? A Rawlsian approach to moral
    motivation, *Business Ethics Quarterly* 12(1): 57–72

Van Buren, H., III 2001. If fairness is the problem, is consent the solution?
    Integrating ISCT and stakeholder theory, *Business Ethics Quarterly*
    11(3): 481–99

Velamuri, S. and Venkataraman, S. 2005. Why stakeholder and stockholder
    theories are not necessarily contradictory: A Knightian insight, *Journal
    of Business Ethics* 61(3): 249–62

Weale, A. 2007. *Democracy*. 2nd edn. Basingstoke, Palgrave

Wijnberg, N. 2000. Normative stakeholder theory and Aristotle: The link
    between ethics and politics, *Journal of Business Ethics* 25(4): 329–42

Williamson, O. 1975. *Markets and Hierarchies: Analysis and Antitrust
    Implications*. New York, Free Press

Williamson, O. 1985. *The Economic Institutions of Capitalism*. New York,
    Free Press

Williston, S. 1888. History of the law of business corporations before 1800
    (I), *Harvard Law Review* 2(3): 105–24

World Business Council for Sustainable Development 1999. Corporate
    social responsibility: Meeting changing expectations. Online at:
    www.wbcsd.org.

Index